JOHN TRENT, Ph.D.

Strong Families in Stressful Times

HARVEST HOUSE PUBLISHERS

EUGENE, OREGON

Cover by Koechel Peterson & Associates, Inc., Minneapolis, Minnesota

Cover photo by Rubberball Photography

Published in association with the literary agency of Alive Communications, Inc., 7680 Goddard Street, Ste 200, Colorado Springs, CO 80920.

STRONG FAMILIES IN STRESSFUL TIMES
Copyright © 2002/2004 by John Trent, Ph.D.
Published by Harvest House Publishers
Eugene, Oregon 97402
www.harvesthousepublishers.com

Trent, John T.
  Strong families in stressful times/John Trent.
    p. cm.
Rev. ed. of: The light of home.
Includes bibliographical references (p.   ).
  ISBN 0-7369-1282-7
  1. Family—Religious life. 2. Family—Religious aspects—Christianity. I. Trent, John T. Light of home. II. Title.
  BV4526.3.T75 2004
  242—dc22   2003017229

Printed in China

04 05 06 07 08 09 10 11 /RDS-KB/ 10 9 8 7 6 5 4 3

Contents

Opening Thoughts:

THE CHOICE WE MUST MAKE...

It was during the tragedy, sadness, and terrible loss of life that marked our American Civil War that President Abraham Lincoln observed, "The strength of our country lies in the homes of our people." That is absolutely true today. Our world was rocked by the acts of terror that began on September 11, 2001, and ever since then our view of what's most important has changed dramatically. In particular, Americans have awoken once again to how important strong families are in stressful times.

It's still hard for many Americans to believe, but we are now at war with a host of determined enemies. And though these terrorists who hate our way of life operate in darkness, their goals have nothing to do with subtlety and shadow. When terrorists strike, their acts of hatred are carefully planned so they can be seen in the brightest light. Their strategy is to fill our eyes—and then our hearts—with unforgettable pictures. And it is from these terrible pictures that they hope to destroy our resolve and strike fear into our hearts.

Terrorists' Pictures Are Meant to Make Us Lose Heart

Listen to these penetrating words that reflect the manipulative power that terrorists seek to wield in our lives:

> A hundred petty crimes or petty accidents will not strike the imagination of crowds in the least, whereas a single great crime or a single great accident will profoundly impress them, even though the results be infinitely less disastrous than the hundreds of small, accidents put together.

> The epidemic of influenza, which caused the death of five thousand persons in Paris alone a few years ago, made very little impression on the popular imagination. *Yet an accident causing the death of only five hundred persons, but all on the same day and in public, as the outcome of the fall, for instance, of the Eiffel Tower, would have produced, on the contrary, an immense impression on the imagination of the crowd.*[1]

These aren't the words of an al-Qaeda operative or Osama bin Laden himself. They were written by Frenchman Gustave le Bon *115 years ago!*

His book *The Crowd: A Study of the Popular Mind* has been called a "timeless handbook" on how to manipulate and brainwash people. In fact, it matches nearly line for line the tactics employed by today's terrorists and the pictures they want to paint in people's minds.

As if to prove le Bon's point, more than 35,000 people are killed each year on our nation's highways. More than 300,000 die each year from lung and throat cancer caused by smoking cigarettes. Yet these individual losses, spread out by geography and occurring incrementally, do not bring the collective sense of loss that comes with a single great tragedy.

Far from being unschooled or unsophisticated, terrorists understand the "picture power" that a major disaster has on the public's imagination. They know the words "This news just breaking!" mean that every major network will immediately begin broadcasting as much live audio and video footage from the scene as possible. They count on replays of a horrific event and endless commentary by political pundits and quickly-called "experts."

With pictures of catastrophe, terrorists seek to demoralize and ultimately defeat us by plunging our country into panic, withdrawal, and inaction. Note the words of Osama bin Laden in his first video broadcast

THOUGH THESE TERRIBLE PICTURES HAVE
THE POWER TO SHOCK AND SADDEN US,
THEY MUST NOT DEFINE US.

after the World Trade Center bombing: "America is full of fear from its north to its south, from its west to its east. Thank God for that."

To be certain, seeing the Pentagon awash in flames and suffocating clouds of dust swallowing up streets and people fleeing from the falling World Trade Center Towers left an unnerving and unforgettable image. But though these terrible pictures have the power to shock and sadden us, they must not define us.

In fact, it is how we react to the pictures we've been handed—and we will be handed more terrible pictures in the future—that will prove to be the challenge of our times and of each American family.

The Pictures We Must Preserve

Exactly one month to the day after the World Trade Center Towers collapsed, at a podium near the still-smoldering ruins, New York Mayor Rudolph Giuliani addressed police officers, firefighters, rescue personnel, and construction workers. Speaking to these heroes—and to the rest of us—the mayor urged all Americans to see beyond the terrible pictures.

"Look at the determination you see around you. Don't look at these ruins. Look at the resolve filling our great city and nation. Don't look at the shock of the moment, but the strength that has come from this terrible event."

Mayor Giuliani was absolutely right. The way out of the fear and confusion so many still feel won't be found in watching slow-motion replays of kidnapped planes being swallowed up by twin 110-story buildings. Nor will you find the fate of our nation lying in the tons of twisted steel and pulverized concrete left behind at the Pentagon or in a field in Pennsylvania.

In fearful, troubling times like these, I'm convinced our eyes need to turn to pictures that highlight the best of our nation.

We can take comfort in the paintings an
tographs of historical events from America's pas
show us the courage and resolve other Americans ...s-
played in times of adversity. Pictures like Emanuel
Leutze's painting of General George Washington
crossing the Delaware River. This revered painting of
courage captures a freezing night when Washington
and his victory-starved army surprised the British and
Hessian troops on the day after Christmas in 1776. Or
photographs like the hurried snapshot of a handful
of Marines raising a flag over Iwo Jima as the battle
raged below—an enduring image of American
heroism replicated when New York City firefighters
raised a flag in the midst of the World Trade Center
rubble.

Yet, perhaps in a surprising way, it is not the pictures of battle, but the pictures of enduring American
beauty—and especially pictures of home—that may be
the greatest help in healing our wounds and giving us
strength of heart.

In Trying Times, We Need to Concentrate on the Right Pictures

Our deepest passions of patriotism, family, and faith
are awakened by pictures of stunning American land-
scapes, of hearth and loving home, of families walking
together on a winter night, and of simpler times in
our country's history.

In times of great trial and loss, we've known this
truth instinctively. Soldiers, sailors, airmen, and Marines
caught up in a foreign war have drawn on these pictures of America to sustain them through battle. For

~~~

WE CAN TAKE COMFORT IN...
HISTORICAL EVENTS FROM AMERICA'S PAST
THAT SHOW US THE COURAGE AND
RESOLVE OTHER AMERICANS DISPLAYED
IN TIMES OF ADVERSITY.

~~~

the Navajo code talkers in World War II, it was the longing to see the sun setting over a red-hued Arizona desert mesa. For a Vietnam veteran surrounded for 13 months by a triple-canopy green jungle, it was the memory of fall leaves of Upper Michigan turning dazzling shades of wine-colored burgundies mingled with saffron, honey, and gold. For a Desert Storm soldier staring at countless waves of sand dunes, it was the longing to see rows of narrow, red-brick houses lining a rain-slick Chicago street.

Today, it's the sailor or airman or woman on the flight deck of a carrier in the Persian Gulf longing to see fields being planted; or for a Marine looking up at the mountains of Afghanistan, or a soldier in the desert cities of Iraq, it's remembering a family trip to Colorado as a child.

As one combat veteran poignantly observed, being constantly surrounded by terrible pictures during wartime exchanges one kind of "normal" for another. "In war you learn survival skills to fit an extreme situation, but in the long run they are not life skills. So if a GI is ever to go back to a 'normal' life, he needs to hear about the church bake sale, who won the big high school football game, and what clever trick the family dog has learned."

Now, with the battle being carried to our shores, it's as if each American has awoken in a war zone. In order to get back to some kind of a "new normal," I'm convinced that it will be the everyday things—the everyday pictures of America—that will renew our resolve and restore to us a sense of reality.

What follows are ten positive "pictures"—ten timeless principles that can specifically show you how to have a home full of light. Each chapter is a reflection or a principle or a truth that American families in each generation tried in their most difficult, darkest hours and found to be true.

As you turn each page, it's my hope that two things will take place in your heart. I pray that each of these ten images and ideas will not only help you experience the title of this book—*Strong Families in Stressful Times*—but will help you live up to a Presidential Proclamation issued less than two weeks after the terrorist attacks.

On September 24, 2001, President George W. Bush issued a stirring proclamation for the families of America, which began with these words:

Strong families make a strong America.

Our president's words remind us that the way to move forward in times of great trial and pain is to draw together with our loved ones. When it comes to homeland defense, *we can fight back each day against the enemies of our freedoms by drawing closer to our family*. In the days to come, some will be called on to serve in foreign and domestic battles. But every American can learn more about living out the words "strong families make a strong America."

For now, more than ever, we need such encouragement.

Now, more than ever, we need to live courageous, caring, meaningful lives.

And now, more than ever...our country needs strong families.

Making Your Family Stronger

In each chapter (each "picture" of a strong family) that follows, I'll close with a short story or discussion point aimed at moving us from theory to application in our homes. For example, *you may be married* and wanting to not just endure another year together, but to experience the kind of closeness you know deep inside is possible.

- ∞ To look into your loved one's eyes and see them light up when you walk in the door.

- ∞ To have her respond to your touch without pulling away.

- ∞ To have him verbally appreciate your efforts on the job and/or around the house.

- ∞ To discover guidelines that ignite or rekindle affection, commitment, or acts of everyday caring—even after ten years and two (or more) kids.

It's my prayer that the principles and "pictures" that follow will help you do just that.

You may be a parent looking for the ability to see once again the value in a challenging child, or you may be someone who needs a "picture" of hope that shows you that you can overcome a rough background and indeed be a blessing to your son or daughter. *Or perhaps you're a single person who wants to build a foundation for a strong family* of your own—one that is different than the sinking sand you've seen in too many homes.

I realize that in today's harsh world of divorce courts, restraining orders, and broken dreams, such talk can seem like fantasy and hyperbole. But with God's love giving you the strength and hope you need—and the right pictures to follow—you can build a love that in each new season of life is as fresh and refreshing as spring.

To help in this process, below are a few suggestions to follow in the Making Your Family Stronger section at the end of each chapter.

First, if you're engaged or married, make the reading of this book a "tag team" affair with your spouse or fiancé. Don't rush through the book as if you're the top student in a speed-reading class. As it is, we're way too hurried as people and couples. Linger on chapters or even paragraphs that hit home. Take time to talk about the stories that touched you or the principles that challenged you. If your spouse simply won't read through the book with you, don't put it down. Read through each picture yourself, knowing you'll be a more loving, caring person or parent as a result—something that can help you emotionally, physically, and spiritually in each day to come.

If you're a single parent or person, I'd challenge you to pick a close friend or family member as a "book buddy." Do what a good friend of ours did and buy a Starbucks or local coffee shop gift card to "reward" your friend and yourself for meeting. Then, in the amount of time it takes to enjoy a single cup of coffee (or, if you're like my wife, a white chocolate mocha, light shot, extra whip, extra ice, Frappuccino—alias "a candy bar in a cup"), share with your friend what you've learned in that one chapter. Ask them to share their thoughts and wisdom as well.

And finally, married or single, when you're finished with this book, I would challenge you to pick a family in your neighborhood or an extended family member who, for whatever reason, is struggling far more than you. Share your book with them, or get them their own book, and then sit down with them and talk through each chapter—as you walk alongside them.

WHEN YOU'RE FINISHED WITH THIS BOOK,
PICK A FAMILY AND SHARE WHAT
YOU'VE LEARNED WITH THEM.

I believe if you strengthen your family—and then reach out to just one other—you'll be doing something "great" for our country. Let me explain by sharing a true story about our sixteenth president.

During the Civil War, President Abraham Lincoln took to attending a midweek church service. In the midst of these terrible days of sacrifice and sorrow, this short time of praise, prayer, and teaching offered comfort and solace to Lincoln's soul. On those Wednesday nights, the president of the United States and an aide who accompanied him would quietly, unobtrusively slip through a side door of the New York Presbyterian Church. More often than not, other people in the congregation were not even aware of his presence.

One night, apparently deeply moved by the message and time of worship, Lincoln stayed seated, quietly reflecting until long after the rest of the parishioners had left. Finally breaking the silence, the adjutant who had accompanied him leaned over and asked him, "Mr. President, what did you think of the sermon?"

After contemplating the question, Lincoln answered, "I thought it was well thought through, powerfully delivered, and very eloquent."

"Then you thought it was a great sermon," his companion replied.

"No," said Lincoln. "I thought it failed."

Finally answering the confused look on his aide, he concluded, *"It failed because the pastor did not ask of us something great."*[2]

I can assure you that as you read and work through the ten "pictures" of a strong family that follow, this book won't "fail" because it hasn't asked "something great" of you. Being a strong family—a "Home of Light" in these dark times—is indeed a great challenge. And so too is the challenge to reach out and help just one hurting family by walking across the street and sharing some of what we've learned.

May the reading of this book, lived out in daily life, be a great experience for you and your family.

The First Picture

Untying the Knots

I ran across some amazing information on New Year's resolutions that show just how much people's goals have changed as a result of what's happened to our country.

For decades, pollsters have contacted people on New Year's Eve and asked them the question: "What's your number one New Year's resolution this year?" Most polling centers, including the Gallup Organization, have conducted yearly surveys and found that the most often heard response is always the same. Can you guess what it would be?

That's right: "I'm going to lose weight this year!"

But after 9/11, not only did our world change, but so did the number one New Year's resolution. On December 31, 2001, and again in 2002, the top vote getter wasn't to lose weight. It was:

"I want to have a closer family."

That's a wonderful resolution, and it's tremendous that in our country, at least on the day this poll was taken, we were more concerned with the loved ones we hold dear than the pounds we hold near. But how do we keep this truly laudable goal of having a stronger family from the usual fate of all our other New Year's resolutions? In other words, how can we keep our goal of growing closer to others from evaporating as quickly as our promise to "never eat another donut" or to "get up at 5:00 A.M. to exercise every day"?

How can we have a strong family in these stressful times—beginning today?

Let me suggest that for most people, the first step forward begins by taking one step back.

Taking One Step Back to Take Many Steps Forward as a Family

Now, if you have a perfect family—the kind that never argues, never gets their feelings hurt, and where everyone always does the right thing in regards to loving and serving each other—then you can feel free to skip ahead to the next chapter. (But before you do, ask your spouse or children if they agree with just how perfect you are!)

For the other 99.9 percent of us who try hard but sometimes fail at being the parent or grandparent, husband or wife, son or daughter we really want to be—it's time to ask some hard questions.

It's Time to Ask Ourselves Hard Questions

Though the "perfect" family is impossible to come by, some people still put that kind of unrealistic expectation on pastors and their families. However, these committed servants struggle just as much as anyone else when it comes to having a strong family. Take a good friend who shared a touching story with me recently.

This pastor recounted how he had rushed home from his church one night in order to eat dinner. Few words were spoken at the table, however, as he sat with his wife and their teenage son and daughter. He was lost in thought as he mentally reviewed his day while wolfing down his food in order to head off to yet another evening commitment.

"I gotta run," my friend announced, without making eye contact with anyone in the family. "It's Tuesday night and that means I've got to go make my visitation calls." As he got up to leave, he heard his daughter's voice.

"Dad," she said, "can I ask you a question before you go?"

"Sure, honey," he said, turning back to look at her.

"Daddy, next week, can you visit our family?"

You can imagine the heartache that flooded over this father. Here he was trying to grow a church, going the extra mile by going out at night to visit the sick and shut-ins. He was working hard to do the right thing...but had to face the fact that when it came to his family, his absence caused his children to feel like orphans at home.

To my friend's credit, he walked back to the table, sat down, and canceled his plans to got out that evening. Instead, beginning with his daughter, he went around the table, asking questions and finding out to his amazement that his son and wife felt the same. They all felt he was never there for them.

"That was the hardest conversation I've ever had with my family or anyone," he told me, "but it turned out to be the absolute best. That night I told them how sorry I was for not being there for them, and I asked what I could do differently—*that's when things began to change...*"

My friend was fortunate to have a daughter willing to risk hurting or upsetting her father to tell him the truth. (As was she, to have a father with a good enough heart to listen to her concerns.)

Great Relationships Begin with Those Willing to "Untie the Knot"

There is an oft-quoted Bible verse that reads, "You will know the truth, and the truth will set you free" (John 8:32 NIV). The Greek word for "to set free" is interesting. It literally means "to untie the knot," and it's the same word that is translated elsewhere, "forgiveness."

Do you get the "picture" that this word carries?

What I'm suggesting in this first look at what it takes to have a close-knit home is that, in order to deal with anger and indifference in a home, you need truth and forgiveness. Anger ties people in knots and indifference puts a double knot on top and cinches it tight. But facing the truth and being willing to ask for forgiveness—and giving it when it's asked of us—"unties the knots" and sets us free to really connect closely with others.

Three Little Words...

My friend Dr. Joe White is the head of six tremendous youth camps near Branson, Missouri. Each summer thousands of teenagers attend these camps.

One year Joe gave each camper a survey, and on it was the question: "What would you most like to hear from your parents?"

The answer the staff received back from several thousand high school students surprised them. In writing the survey, the counselors were certain that what most teenagers would like to hear were the three words, "I love you." But while those are three great words to say to any teenager, they weren't the words these kids most wanted to hear.

Actually, they wanted to hear two words, not three. "I'm sorry."

Those are often tough words for a parent to say. Do you know what it takes for an electrical light to turn on? You have to have a closed circuit. If you have an open loop in the circuit—a break in the wiring— the light never goes on. The same thing is true for a family. The reason so many homes never light up from the inside is that there are breaks in the circuit. Open loops.

Forgiveness helps close loops and lights up homes. So here's a practical, challenging assignment if you're serious about lighting up your home with God's love and your own. Don't wait for your spouse or son or daughter to stop you at the dinner table to tell you that things need to change. Don't wait for your parents or a sibling to show up at your doorstep and say, "I'm sorry. It was my fault."

Put away the pride that says, "It's not my problem" or "That's just the way I am" or "It was their fault" and remember something important.

The stronger person initiates the peace.

The stronger person is the one willing to untie the knots.

And a strong family requires a willingness for people to say when they are wrong, "I'm sorry. What can I do to make things better, or to be a better person?"

I know that asking people to admit they were wrong and to take responsibility to make things right is rather a hard way to start this book. But I never said that having a strong family was going to be easy. In fact, I'll be the first to admit that it goes against my grain to have to admit when I'm wrong. But I've learned that it doesn't cause me to lose ground in my marriage or with our daughters when I do. *In fact, the opposite is true.* I gain ground as a husband and father, and I become a model for my children when I exhibit the strength it takes to assume personal responsibility for wrong actions that includes saying, "I'm sorry. How can I make this right?"

A STRONG FAMILY REQUIRES A WILLINGNESS FOR PEOPLE TO SAY WHEN THEY ARE WRONG, "I'M SORRY. WHAT CAN I DO TO MAKE THINGS BETTER, OR TO BE A BETTER PERSON?"

In a later chapter, we'll talk about how to come to grips with someone (like a parent) who never will say they're sorry or admit they're wrong. But we don't have to stay tied up in "knots" ourselves. We can be persons strong enough to forgive and say "we're sorry." We can open doors we may have shut.

For now, more than ever, we need to face past hurts and take responsibility.

Making Your Family Stronger

Whatever metaphor you use—clearing the deck, going back to the starting line, rebooting, blasting before you build—when we lay aside the encumbrances that keep us from connecting with our loved ones, we're at the right place to begin building a strong family.

In this chapter, the challenge was laid out to "untie the knots" we've caused in our relationships. But what if we choose *not* to untie the knots? Or perhaps even more helpful to discuss, how can we tell if we've still got knots that need untying in our family relationship? For those serious about having a strong family, let's look at three warning signs.

1. If the intensity of anger over present mistakes doesn't match a realistic response, you've got knots to untie.

Read and discuss the following example.

Growing up, Phil watched his mother recklessly spend every dime that came her way. Unlike many single parents, Phil's mother had inherited a significant amount of money in a trust fund that she could dip into each year (a trust account she controlled totally by age 35). Yet instead of saving or investing, she put great strain on her family with major spending binges; so much so that at times even the basics were unavailable for the children. Phil's memories were of carrying a ripped backpack to grade school when two closets were jammed with his mother's new clothes. He also recalls his mother going to elaborate dinners at a fancy restaurant while he made peanut butter sandwiches for himself and his sister. Phil's mother died when he was still in high school, and even then he faced the fallout of her "spending" problems. Unknown to him, she had also illegally raided the college funds the grandparents had set aside for each child, as well as running up tremendous credit card debt. Forget the private school he had the grades and desire to attend. Phil worked full-time while going to the local college he could barely afford.

That was a "past" issue for Phil, but he's still fighting it today. If Phil's wife, Diane, goes over budget for food by even a few dollars—and even for a good reason— Phil responds with an earthquake of emotions. When spending forty dollars more than they've budgeted for a child's birthday party should barely register on the emotional Richter scale, Phil responds with a 7.1 quake! That's because he isn't reacting to a present problem alone; he's dragging in wells of emotions from the past. In effect, he's yelling at his mother every time he's shouting at Diane.

Discuss what will happen if Phil doesn't deal with his anger toward his mother—untie the knots with her—even though she's passed away. Just what would it take, from your reading of this story, for him to untie the knot with his mom? What knots do you think he may have to untie with his wife as well? To make your family stronger, what are the issues you see in your relationships from the past that can cause "knots" in the present?

2. If you find yourself adding physical distance when you communicate, you've got knots to untie.

Think about a recent argument you've had with your spouse or a close friend. Were you sitting across the room or standing on opposite sides of an "island" in the kitchen when hurtful words started to fly? Realize it or not, clinical studies show that the distance you put between yourself and the person you're trying to communicate with is a good indication of the emotional distance in the relationship. You will see meaningful communication decrease as the distance (and volume level) between you and the person you're arguing with increases.

It may seem a small thing to sit next to your spouse. But try getting close to someone when you, or that person, are all tied up in knots. Take a hard look at the distance between you as you talk. Is there a knot you need to untie, caused by "distance," that is holding you back from coming close today?

3. If you've "heard it all before" your spouse or child finish a thought, you've got knots to untie.

In almost every marriage, there is one person who is "quicker to the draw" when it comes to framing verbal messages. Yet Proverbs 18:13 points out a lasting truth—"He who gives an answer before he hears, it is folly and shame to him." If you feel as though you already know *exactly* what your loved one is going to say—and you consistently interrupt or overreact to something he or she says, even before they finish talking—you've got knots to untie. Even if he or she has said the same thing 8,000 times, perhaps there's a reason the issue has come up those 7,999 times before. Have your loved one rate you as a listener—and be ready to untie the knot if you find your spouse doesn't feel as though he or she has a chance to finish a thought before you give an answer.

The Second Picture

CARVING OUT TIME FOR CLOSENESS

*B*ut you just don't understand!" she told me. "It's not going to work. I'm sick of trying. It hasn't gotten any better."

These were the words of a woman who came into my counseling office with her husband. Not that she *wanted* to come into the office, mind you. But her father, who was paying for her divorce attorney, said he wouldn't pay a cent to her lawyer unless she came for counseling first. Which meant I was told I had four sessions to change things between them or she was gone.

Four sessions isn't much time, so I decided to take up a good part of the first session by reading her a story. Now if that sounds to you like wasting good time in the face of a looming deadline or a lack of due diligence on the part of a counselor...well, that's just what she said! But that was before she heard the story.

What follows is something that turned this couple's relationship around. It may not seem as though it has a lot to do with having a strong family when you begin to read it...but look closer. It's actually a beautiful scene, painted by a master artist, that captures the second picture of a strong family I'd like to share with you.

"Why Bother...It's Never Going to Work"

The winter of 1498 was memorable for its bitter cold. The city of Florence, Italy, was blanketed in snow, and Michelangelo Buonarroti's heart was as heavy as the gray clouds that dipped low and blocked out the sun.

The Grand Duke of Florence, Lorenzo de Medici, had been the young artist's benefactor. It was this great supporter of the arts who had given Michelangelo the numerous slabs of marble he needed to refine his incredible talents. But before Michelangelo was able to create many of his masterpieces, his source of marble was cut off.

The old duke died, and his son, Piero, had no use for a sculptor on the payroll. That went double for wasting good money on marble. So the artist's great talents were put on the shelf, and Michelangelo sat and waited. That is, until a few days before a great party at the new duke's palace.

In what looked like an incredible answer to his prayers, Michelangelo was summoned before Piero. He'd never been to the palace, even when the Grand Duke had been alive, and he hurried down the streets, past the guards, and in to see Duke Piero.

While he was afraid to believe it, the rumor circulated by the servant who came to fetch Michelangelo was that he was being commissioned to carve a great statue! At last!

When Michelangelo arrived at the palace, he was ushered into a large room where not only Duke Piero de Medici stood but also a crowd of the duke's friends. He was indeed told that his services as a sculptor were needed by his new patron. All he had to do was to go down to the garden, and he'd find all the white marble he needed to make a masterpiece for the duke's party.

Can you guess by now what the duke was actually asking Michelangelo to do? All the white marble in the garden was...snow. Perhaps the greatest sculptor of all time had been brought to the palace to create a snow sculpture for a royal dinner party!

Just imagine for a moment what was going through Michelangelo's mind as he walked from the room and down to the garden. If it had been me, I'd have been furious. What an embarrassment! What a colossal waste of time—to put all that effort into something that would melt as soon as the sun broke through the clouds!

Michelangelo could have stormed out or at least left the duke's presence with an angry, unwilling heart. Instead, he simply went to work. Hour after hour he gathered snow into a great mound. Then, at last, he began to carve.

Working with the packed snow from the top down (when normally with stone you carve from the base on up), a head appeared, and then shoulders, limbs, torso, and legs. A figure was emerging from the white snow that would be viewed as a joke by Duke Piero and his guests, and then melt away in no time.

Yet still, Michelangelo worked. That's because he had decided in his heart that even if all he could do was make Florence a more beautiful place for a few hours—he would put all his heart into carving that block of snow. And then it came time for Piero's party.

The guests arrived. The snow carving finally was unveiled...and instead of laughter came breathless silence. The duke and his guests were staring in awe and amazement at the figure in the snow that seemed able to breathe and walk and even sling a rock at a giant. For that statue made of snow was created by Michelangelo to represent the Bible's David.

IN GOD'S EYES, EVERY SINGLE ACT OF
FAITHFULNESS IS NOTED.

The duke was silenced by the tireless efforts of the young artist who had created a masterpiece made out of snow.

Then, amazingly, that statue turned to marble.

Not that hour of course, for it wasn't magic. But in the days that followed, Michelangelo's *David* was replicated in marble—given him by none other than Duke Piero himself. This priceless work has drawn millions of people to Florence—all because Michelangelo was willing to carve something of beauty out of snow....

Carving Snow Statues

Which—I'm sure you were waiting for this—brings us to the second picture of a strong family and the effect this story had on that young woman in my office.

Nearly every day, people walk into my counseling office feeling as though they're wasting their time carving snow statues. Why bother to put effort into a relationship that's doomed to fail? Why try so hard when all the talking and praying and trying we're doing is just going to melt when things heat up.

Why bother to try—after all, it's just snow.

That's also what it can seem like for the person who tries to do an excellent job for a boss who doesn't appreciate his or her efforts. Or for parents who work so hard to raise kids who never seem to say thanks. Or for the high school student who is tempted to quit practicing when she's stuck on third string on the basketball team. Or the grown child who spends countless hours taking care of an aging parent who gives zero thanks.

Do our efforts matter?

Absolutely—because God always rewards faithfulness.

The effort you put into building a strong family, or continuing to work on a struggling marriage, or increasing your faith, or creating something as lasting as you can at work, may seem as though you're carving snow—but in God's eyes, every single act of faithfulness is noted. You're carving marble to Him when you stay faithful even when it's tough

You can take King David's word on that. "To the faithful You show yourself faithful," says the shepherd-turned-king in Psalm 18:25 (NIV).

God hangs out with faithful people—even if all they think they're accomplishing while they're here on earth is carving in the snow.

Week two after hearing this story was when that woman in my office began to hope that her marriage could be better after all. Actions influence feelings, so as she put her whole heart into really trying—as did her husband—she found herself actually relaxing inside. By week three, acts of service had led to a grudging respect. By week four, that respect had turned to like, and for the next eight weeks (which they paid for), that like turned back into the love they thought they had lost.

That's the second picture of what it takes to have a strong family. The courage, character, hope, and faith to keep trying—even if we think all our efforts are in vain. God rewards such efforts. In this life and in the next.

May each of us be faithful today in doing our best with the "snow" we're given—for now, more than ever, we need the marble of faithfulness to build strong families.

Making Your Family Stronger

In this chapter the need to stay faithful and realize that God sees and rewards our "efforts" was stressed. Yet in real life, is effort always rewarded? Read the story that follows and discuss your thoughts on faithfulness and the way immediate appreciation isn't always linked with effort.

Growing up in a single-parent home, I never had a father to instruct me in using tools or working on cars. That meant I entered our marriage somewhat "mechanically challenged"—particularly in comparison to Cindy's father and brothers. They rebuilt engines, did all their own brake, maintenance, and body work, and could repair the Mars Rover if called on, I'm sure.

It's with that background that Cindy insisted I change the oil in our car to save money when we were first married. She did that right after we watched a television commercial for Valvoline oil where they actually had a monkey do an oil change!

Inspired and challenged, I went next door that Saturday afternoon and borrowed a number of tools from my very patient neighbor. Did I ask for instructions on changing the oil? Absolutely not! That would have been a sign of weakness in my book. Instead, I crawled under the car and discovered that right in front of my eyes was a very large bolt.

Taking my wrench, I unscrewed the bolt and out came gushing "red" oil. I thought to myself, "Boy, it's a good thing I'm changing the oil because it must turn red when it gets really old."

Cindy was shocked when I walked back in the house in less than an hour, all washed up and the car filled up with new Valvoline oil. Of course, as you might imagine, she wasn't really as shocked then as she was when our car began to smoke and shake— and finally freeze up—on Central Expressway in Dallas the next morning on our way to church.

You couldn't fault my "effort" in draining out all the transmission fluid and replacing it with oil...or could you? Which leads to the following questions I'd like you to discuss.

Has there been a time in your marriage (hopefully not as dramatic) when you felt you put effort into something to please your spouse and the result simply wasn't what you expected? What do you think happens to us inside when we feel as though we're a failure? Or that our efforts don't count?

On the other hand, what does faithfulness have to do with staying committed and positive—even when we make a mistake?

When Shannon Sharpe, the All-Pro tight end for the Denver Broncos, was asked what most impressed him about their new quarterback at the beginning of the 2003 football season, Jake Plummer, he said, "He's never down, never. Make a bad play? All right, let's get 'em next time. Don't pout. *To be a great player, you have to have a short memory. You can't dwell on it and say, 'I'm going to sulk for a while.' You have to come back and make up for it the next time.* That's what he does. He's always positive, always. I like that."[3]

That's not just a description of a great quarterback. That's a picture of someone like Michelangelo, who kept carving in the snow—and of a spouse who keeps trying and working to make things better in his or her marriage—even if he burns up the transmission.

The Third Picture

A MARRIAGE MARKED BY SERVING AND SHARING

I can remember that day as though it were yesterday. The light was streaming in on a beautiful late-spring morning when I opened my eyes. There were only a few weeks left in the semester before final exams...and then the freedom of a summer with no graduate school. I woke up in a good mood and walked down the hall into the kitchen, thinking Cindy, my precious wife of only two years at the time, would already be up and have started the coffee.

She was up all right, but she hadn't spent her time making lattes or a big breakfast. Instead, she was getting ready to serve me a picture I've never forgotten in 25 years of marriage.

There in the kitchen, just on the left as I walked in, was the little dinette set we'd bought at an auction. It wasn't worthy of the name antique, even though it did have a semi-50s look with plastic and chrome. What I noticed was actually on the table. There, where I normally sat, was a plate with one of my textbooks on it that I'd been studying for finals.

It was a large book. It was the only thing sitting on the table—and it was dramatically placed on a plate. Even I couldn't miss the fact that this must have been put there purposefully by my bride.

So I took the bait.

"What's this?" I asked, smiling. "Is it a new study technique? Digesting your textbooks for breakfast to make you smarter?"

"No," my wise wife said, "this is how I feel about our relationship. I could have picked any of your textbooks, but this is how I feel about our marriage right now."

Seeing I was not getting her meaning, she went on.

"Right now you're studying really hard, John. That's kind of like how you were when we were dating. You spent lots of time getting to know me. You'd look ahead with me, like you couldn't wait to turn the page and see what was next. You took me seriously. But then we got married, and I began to feel like I was one of your books after final exams. It goes up on the shelf, you get busy with other things, and I'm left there with all your other books..."

Needless to say, I got the picture that morning.

In fact, I doubt whether she could have picked a better book to put on my plate. Every time I picked up that textbook between that morning and final exams, I thought again about her words. They haunted me. They made me feel ashamed. Here I was, married only two years—and in the middle of my doctoral program in marriage and family counseling—and I'd succeeded in making my wife feel like a used, ignored textbook. Some great counselor I was going to be.

Have you ever been there?

On either side of the table?

It was so confusing at the time. We'd had such a great courtship. We hardly had any tense discussions, much less big arguments. It seemed as though we couldn't spend enough time together talking. But that morning, I had to admit deep inside that Cindy was right. I couldn't even become defensive or angry or think of a "cute" comeback. I just said I was sorry, and I asked her to sit down at that nearly worthless table to talk about how we could make our relationship priceless and valuable again.

Let's Go Out to the Movies

I didn't know back then—I didn't have a clue back then—what real intimacy in a marriage looked like. Now, *courtship,* that was different. I could do courtship. That's because I'd seen countless movies that pictured courtship and read the occasional book where guy meets girl—though mostly war novels where the guy marches away. Even today, little has changed when it comes to the movies. From *You've Got Mail* to *How to Lose a Guy in 10 Days* or any one of a hundred different romance "flicks" you'll find basically the same premise. Namely, the hard work of the relationship is the courtship.

According to the big screen, it's getting the person to marry you that's the biggest challenge. You assume from watching how happy they are that things will go like a dream from there. But neither by watching movies nor in real life (particularly as I grew up in a single-parent household) did I ever see what happens in a warm, loving marriage. I got married like thousands of people like me—not realizing that the real work of maintaining a strong marriage comes after the wedding.

Somehow, I missed the part in *You've Got Mail* where you see Meg Ryan and Tom Hanks learning how to disagree without damaging each other's sense of self-worth. I must have been out of the room when Matthew McConaughey in *How to Lose a Guy in 10 Days* discovered that helping with the dishes and other chores around the house in the morning had a direct link to how romantic things would be at night.

The pictures we're bombarded with in our culture don't prepare us to deal with the emotions of having to cancel our vacation because all our money has to go into a new furnace, or how to face a crop failure, or how to stay close when you have to walk in the door and tell your spouse, "I lost my job" the same week they lost theirs.

There just aren't many pictures of real love on the big screen that portray a close marriage. But that doesn't mean there aren't pictures that can guide us.

The picture I got that morning from Cindy was a wake-up call that I had to work hard on my marriage if I wanted it to grow and last. M. Scott Peck, in his landmark book *The Road Less Traveled,* begins with a simple statement of fact: "Life is hard. Once you accept this fact, it becomes easier." Let me paraphrase that observation for those of us who are married.

"Having a strong marriage is hard work. Once a husband and wife realize they have two full-time jobs—what they do for a living or raising the children or both *and* the full-time effort it takes to keep a marriage strong and growing—things begin to change for the better." But with only four percent of couples having more than one session of premarital counseling, most don't realize this.

THE REAL WORK OF MAINTAINING A STRONG MARRIAGE COMES AFTER THE WEDDING.

Once a husband settles into the fact that he has two full-time jobs, he begins to realize that he isn't coming home just to rest but to relate. Once a wife realizes that blessing and building up her husband is her second full-time job, it changes her inner commitment and caring level. When both partners "get" this concept that serving and sharing and building a marriage requires the commitment of a full-time job, I've seen them actually become more patient with one another. They start asking questions to clarify a position instead of just blasting each other. They're less critical, and they actually start remembering why they love each other.

Put two people working overtime to have a strong marriage—each one committed to making deposits of love and respect into their relationship—and you've got a great place to come home to. Problems and issues and all, it's also a tremendous place for children and grandchildren to be as well.

Ask yourself these questions: If your marriage were a business, would it be making a profit? Would you even be in business? Do you have a business plan for your marriage, or are you just winging it, thinking success comes without effort...just like it does in the movies?

Infatuation takes almost no effort. For example, you might see someone from across the room—like the first time I saw Cindy—and fall head over heels. But intimacy is earned the old-fashioned way. Twenty-five years after I saw Cindy from across a crowded room, we're still in love. Not just because I still think she's beautiful, but because we've both worked full-time to build a strong marriage and keep our home full of light.

Now, more than ever, a strong marriage takes sensitivity, a servant's heart, measured words, and a willingness to commit to building a loving marriage.

And there's one more thing that can give you the strength to get up and do those chores when you'd rather not, to help you volunteer to get the children ready in the morning instead of sitting in the car beeping. It's the same thing that can deepen your love and passion and commitment for your life-partner like nothing else can or will.

A couple who truly loves God will find themselves growing closer, even when the going gets tough. That's because when you look in the Lord's eyes, He keeps reminding you of words such as faithfulness, patience, service, and sacrifice. When you love the Lord, you keep remembering how much He's forgiven you...and you realize it's about time you forgave your spouse for not being perfect. And when couples pray consistently with each other, to the God who knows and loves them, there are dramatically fewer divorces. (That's not just a clinical reality. Just try praying together night after night without getting or staying closer. It's really hard to muster up hate for someone you pray with each night!)

I'm Back in the Kitchen...

Every once in a while when I walk into the kitchen in our house, I look over at our breakfast nook and see the beautiful oak table and chairs Cindy finished herself. That's when I think about the little chrome and plastic table we once had, now long gone, and the morning I was served a textbook for breakfast.

By the way, Cindy only served me a textbook once. That's because a wise, beautiful, woman who still loves me helped me immensely that morning by giving me a picture I'll never forget.

And speaking of pictures, you've just seen the third picture of a strong family. A picture where each spouse commits to the hard daily work of serving and sharing—aided immensely by a love for God—that can build and maintain a lasting relationship.

For now, more than ever, we need strong marriages.

Making Your Family Stronger

This chapter illustrated how important working at serving and sharing are to having a strong marriage in stressful times. How can you live out serving and sharing in practical ways? How about becoming a "spy catcher" in your home? Let me explain by sharing one of my favorite stories from childhood. After you've read it, discuss how it can help you spot areas that can make a real difference in your marriage today.

While World War II was being fought on the beaches in the Pacific and among the hedgerows in Europe, there were encounters with the "enemy" right here on our home soil. As a typical boy, I loved hearing war stories, and especially one that included a member of my own family, Aunt Dovie. When a Nazi spy was hiding in her assembly plant, she actually faced down and caught the culprit!

My aunt, along with thousands of other "Rosie the Riveters," did more than her fair share supporting the war effort. For Aunt Dovie, that meant working in the Allison engine plant near Indianapolis, Indiana. Though barely five feet tall, she pulled five, and sometimes six, ten-hour shifts a week as a shift supervisor. Engine parts for the famous "Flying Fortress" bombers were made at this plant, and Aunt Dovie's job was at the very end of the assembly line. There, beautiful silver-coated pistons were packed into crates to be shipped to England.

There was a tremendous need for spare engine parts to keep the bombers in the air, but something terrible was happening. When these crucial engine parts finally arrived in England and were uncrated, they were covered with pin-sized holes. The pockmarks on the pistons rendered them useless—a clear act of sabotage!

Tracing back the sabotaged parts all the way to Aunt Dovie's Indiana plant, the FBI arrived and assembled all the supervisors and staff. They spelled out the problem in no uncertain terms—*there was a spy in their midst!* The authorities believed that someone was splashing acid on the pistons before they were crated and shipped. As you might imagine, every part of the assembly process was scrutinized. Yet new lots arriving in England *continued* to arrive with the same pin-sized holes.

Then, one day, my aunt walked out of the lunchroom—and there right in front of her was the spy! She hurried to find her supervisor, and sure enough, it turned out Aunt Dovie had spotted the Nazi culprit. The cunning spy who had ruined so many crucial engine parts was none other than...the salted peanut machine just outside the cafeteria door. Workers were grabbing handfuls of peanuts and then going back to work without washing their hands. Tiny grains of salt left on the pistons during the long journey to England created the pin-sized holes.

And what does this story about being a spy-catcher have to do with having a strong marriage? Actually a great deal. For in every marriage, it is the "little irritants" that, if ignored, over time can ruin a relationship. (For instance, not watching our tone of voice, failing to follow through on promised tasks, "forgetting" to praise, or dismissing someone's thoughts, feelings, or fears is like putting salt on a piston). And it's the "small" acts of serving and sharing that can add up to a great relationship (as in anticipating a loved one's need and offering to help, praising something they do right, affirming them in front of others, or asking the question, "What can I do to make things better?").

In Song of Solomon 2:15, Solomon's bride says to him, "Catch the foxes for us. The little foxes that are ruining the vineyards, while our vineyards are in blossom."

Can you see the parallel between pistons and foxes?

Even when things are going well, there are small things that can nip away at your relationship—in the same way a little bit of salt can eat away at pistons.

So let's get very practical.

Husbands, what are you doing today, in relating to your wife, that is like rubbing salt on a silver piston?

Is your tone of voice loud or harsh when she asks you a question?

Do you consistently back out of promises you've made to help out at home or spend time with the family?

Do you talk about doing something "spiritual" with the kids, but months or even a year has gone by and it's still all talk…no action?

Wives, what are you doing today that, to your husband, is like rubbing salt on a silver piston?

Do you ridicule his efforts at work or compare him to other more "successful" husbands?

Do you withhold positive words or affection because you're waiting for your husband to reach a certain "threshold" before he's earned an act of caring?

Do you focus so much on a child or career that you know in your heart of hearts you take your husband for granted, like a roommate who is there but not a vital part of your life?

What are the "foxes" or small issues that you can spot and then seek to solve? Pick one and commit to dealing with it this week. To have a marriage committed to serving and sharing, you must be proactive in spotting and solving small issues. It's a key way to build a strong family.

The Fourth Picture

"BEING THERE" FOR OUR CHILDREN

*W*hich do you think is safer—driving or flying on a commercial aircraft? Do you think smoking is less dangerous than being around handguns? Or that more Americans die of homicide than suicide? Or that AIDS is more lethal than kidney disease?

If you're like the average American, you answered most of these questions incorrectly. These were the findings of Dr. Paul Slovic at the University of Oregon, who has spent decades studying how we decide what's risky and what isn't. Objective statistics find that driving and smoking and suicide and kidney disease are far more lethal than what they're compared to above. What causes this major difference between the real level of risk and the risk level we feel inside?

Namely, people tend to underestimate risk when they think they're in control. For example, the average person feels more in control and safer in their car than when a pilot is flying them somewhere.

Now what does all that talk of risk have to do with having a strong family—and especially being a loving parent? Actually, a lot more than you might think.

Take the Risk to "Be There" For Your Kids

In a landmark study in *Pediatrics,* the journal of the American Academy of Pediatrics, Dr. James Sargent of Dartmouth Medical School found that parents over-rated another risk factor. Namely, the risk of really engaging their children—especially, as they get older.

"We overrate the rebelliousness of teenagers," said Dr. Sargent.

"That works to our disadvantage...[because] parents underestimate their influence on their children. They have an overly heightened concern about coming down hard on their kids about things like smoking because they think it's going to make them more rebellious. Just the opposite is true."[4]

As we look at our fourth picture of what makes a strong family, we can see another essential for having a home full of light. Namely, it takes loving parents who are willing to "be there" for their children—even if that means facing their fears of rejection and confronting their children on issues of right and wrong.

Particularly when children are young, there's a saying you hear constantly on advertisements that moms and dads should take to heart. "You must be present to win."

Being physically present for a child is absolutely critical. We should make every effort to keep our hobbies from keeping us from our kids. And we should use "other care" as little as humanly possible. But even this may not be enough. I've counseled with hundreds of grown children over the past 25 years who grew up feeling as though their mom or dad was never "there" for them—and yet their parents were always at home.

To be there for a child means much more than just sleeping under the same roof. It means that *our name and our eyes and our hearts are there for them*—always. Let me briefly explain what all that means.

Many years ago, there was an amazing grand opening of sorts. It involved the entire nation of Israel and the dedication of their first Temple. Basically, for years they had housed their precious Ark of the Covenant in a large tent called the Tabernacle. At long last they had a permanent place for the ark. A wonderful temple King Solomon built would now house the ark and become Israel's central place of worship.

But the ceremony and celebration wasn't the best part of the dedication. The best part came after the great Temple had been dedicated. For that was when Almighty God spoke to Solomon and gave him this promise: "I have heard the prayer and plea you have made before me; I have consecrated this temple, which you have built, by putting my Name there forever. My eyes and my heart will always be there" (1 Kings 9:3 NIV).

Can you imagine the security the nation of Israel felt at that time? They finally had a temple and their heavenly Father's word that He wasn't going anywhere. Forever, His name, eyes, and heart would be there for His people.

Let's apply that to loving parents who need to be there for their children today. Namely, those same three things that God promised to His people centuries ago are at the heart of healthy family research today. Let me explain.

Forever—meaning way beyond what is convenient or cultural—our children need to know we have our "name" on them. In olden times, a craftsman would put his name on something to show he was proud of it, and that it was considered worthy to carry his name. Do your children feel that they are of great value to you? Do they know that of all the children in the world you'd put your name on them?

Then there are the eyes we need to have on our children. We need to look for the best in their lives, not the worst. And always, our heart should be there as well. A heart to listen and love, to put ice on boo-boos when they're toddlers and to pray over broken dreams in their teens.

But having our eyes, name, and hearts "be there" are not the only aspects of the job description of a parent who wants a strong family. There's also the need to be strong enough to face up to our children on issues of right and wrong.

Booms in a Child's Bedroom

During my high school years, there were times I can remember feeling my mother was violating my rights when she refused to let my twin brother, Jeff, and me lock our door. (Except when we were changing, of course.) In part, she needed access in order to get clean laundry in and dirty clothes out. But even more—she wanted to make sure we weren't hiding or doing anything in our rooms that we shouldn't be doing.

How dare she! But she dared. And she also let us know that she wouldn't let us lock our doors because, *"If we weren't changing and weren't doing anything wrong, then why couldn't we open the door?"*

At times we ranted and raved…but we never did figure out a good answer to her question. Besides that, she stood fast. And guess what? Even though I was upset with her coming into the room at times, I knew she was right. There were times we *were* tempted to do or bring things into our room that we shouldn't— but with my mom on watch, there was never a safe haven in our home to do wrong.

The reason I share that is because I am amazed at how often a newspaper will note that the police found illegal guns or bomb-making materials in the rooms of murderous teens. When I've heard they've found military grade C-4 or 9mm hollow-point ammunition or homemade explosives in a child's or teenager's room, my first question is, "Where in the world were their parents?"

TO BE THERE FOR A CHILD MEANS…
THAT OUR NAME AND OUR
EYES AND OUR HEARTS ARE THERE FOR
THEM—ALWAYS.

Strong parents in strong families know enough to not let their children lock them out of their lives—or things like drugs, immoral materials, or, for a troubled few, even guns or bombs can end up in hormone-driven or angry kids' rooms at times. It takes effort and courage to face up to our children, at times, and a willingness to face their anger or displeasure when we care enough to confront them in love.

So to live out this fourth picture of a strong family, it takes a loving parent who commits to "forever" having their name, eyes, and heart watch over their child. And as part of "being there," we must have the strength to stand up for what's right and wrong.

ᠬᢧᢧᢧ
Making Your Family Stronger

This chapter shared how important it is to not just be "physically" present for our children, but to "be there" for them emotionally and spiritually as well. That's a challenge, no doubt. But to get even more practical, here are four "checkpoints" that mark parents who are committed to "being there" for their son or daughter. Read through them and then discuss which ones you've done well with—and which ones you could work on.

1. "Being there" for our children starts with how we treat our own parents.

Many of us don't realize that the first of the Ten Commandments with a promise is to "Honor your father and mother…so that it may be well with you, and that you may live long on the earth" (Ephesians 6:2-3). Honoring a parent doesn't mean we excuse wrong behavior if it was there, or that we obey everything a parent says when we're an adult. But it means we treat our parents with "high value." How have you done in "being there" for your parents? Did you know your children watch how you treat your parents as a model for how you'll be treated one day?

Do our children see us "being there" for our parents?

2. "Being there" for our children means helping them find value in difficult times.

In the first chapter of the book of James, we're told that "trials" are inevitable. That's true for our children as well. Part of "being there" for our children is helping them find value in trials—which comes much easier if our children see us doing that. When trials and problems come in your life, do your kids see you looking for lessons learned and staying faithful and positive? Coming alongside your children when they're hurting, with arms willing to hug, ears wanting to listen, and words hoping to encourage, can be a great way of demonstrating you're "there" for them in good times and bad.

Are you a model for your child of how positive lessons can be learned from difficult times?

3. "Being there" for our children helps them see their strengths in a world that focuses on weaknesses.

At my ministry site, www.strongfamilies.com, parents can fill out an online strengths assessment that only takes five to seven minutes, yet emails back a 28-page strengths assessment. In my counseling and conferences, I urge parents to have their children as young as ten take the assessment as well. Why?

Because while it only takes a few minutes to complete, it instantly emails them back 27 pages of why they're so valuable, and one page of what they need to work on as a person. One key aspect of "being there" for children is helping them see their strengths—not just point out their weaknesses.[5]

How are you doing at "being there" to point out your child's strengths?

4. "Being there" for our children is also about establishing loving boundaries.

Each time we make the effort to provide a loving boundary for our children, we not only protect them, we help to produce security and confidence in their lives. In a sense we are "gatekeepers," and when a child sees that we're serious about setting boundaries and enforcing them, it can make a real statement— "What's inside those gates must be very valuable if it's worth protecting." It's tough to be the parent who has to set boundaries in a world with no lines, but a key part of "being there" is to guide, direct, and protect our child. Keep this in mind. Our culture will try to erase childhood by erasing all "boundaries." If nothing is off-limits for a child (from pornographic images to indecent acts), then there is no childhood. "Being there" for a child means keeping things out, not just keeping the child in.

How are you doing at "being there" to set and keep appropriate "boundaries" for your child?

The Fifth Picture

AFFIRMING COURAGE IN OUR CHILDREN

ebecca and Abigail Bates lived in a lighthouse on the coast of Massachusetts near the small village of Scituate. Their father kept the light shining at the harbor entrance to guide ships away from the rock-strewn coast.

One day in 1814, their mother and father left the young girls in charge of the lighthouse while they used their rowboat to reach a nearby village. As the girls performed their assigned chores, they saw a ship come around the point. This wasn't just any ship—it was a British frigate, and America was at war with England. British ships would often try to sneak in using rowboats filled with soldiers to attack villages. In fact, Scituate had already been sacked once, and the British had left ten American ships burning in the harbor.

There were no adults around. Just Rebecca and Abigail. But the village had to be warned. Perhaps the British could be stopped if the sisters found a way to call for help. What happened next saved Scituate and showed incredible bravery.

British rowboats full of soldiers left the frigate and rowed steadily toward shore. But the two girls had done some quick thinking…and praying. They ran into the lighthouse, where Abigail took her father's drum and Rebecca took a fife. They quickly hid themselves in a clump of cedar trees near the shoreline. Just before the soldiers stepped out of their boats, the British heard the beating of a drum and the playing of "Yankee Doodle" on a fife! Thinking the local militia were in hiding and had been called into line to rake the boats with musket fire, the British troops fell over themselves getting back in their rowboats and raced back to the mother ship. The village was saved!

Any parent would be proud if their children displayed Abigail and Rebecca's kind of ingenuity and courage. Thankfully, few children will have to face the kind of danger these two patriot sisters did, but it is important for our sons and daughters to learn how to show courage under fire, even in life's smaller battles.

Affirming Courageous Choices Can Light Up Your Home

As parents, we need to affirm a son who goes and gets a teacher to rescue a friend from a playground bully; or a daughter who keeps working hard to get good grades, even when she is ridiculed by others for being "too smart" or "teacher's pet." We need to affirm the child who shows courage and discipline to come back from a sports injury, or the twins who choose friends that want to do right, not wrong.

Applauding Small Acts of Courage
in Daily Life

The fifth picture of a strong family is affirming courage in our children, even when their acts of bravery may seem small. Take an act of courage that recently took place at a youth basketball game where we live.

A father I know was an All-State athlete when he was young. Today he is his son's coach. Picture a *competitive* person who still is in good enough shape to go out on the court and play. But also picture a father who is wise enough to see a courageous act for what it is and can praise his son for it—even though it cost his team a play-off game.

With under two minutes left in their basketball game and his team up by only one point, there was a scramble for the ball. Ten-year-old Matthew, the coach's son, heard the referee make the call when the ball went out of bounds—"Blue ball!"

Matthew's team had possession! They could run out the clock or run up their lead. But Matthew knew something the referee apparently didn't. He walked over to the referee and said, "I touched the ball last, Ref."

There was a pause as the referee looked intently at him. Then he yelled, "Red ball! Red ball!" and switched possession to the other team.

I realize this was youth league, not the NBA. But I can also picture many coaches, especially many competitive fathers in the coaching ranks, who would have come *unglued* if their son decided to have an integrity attack in the last two minutes of the game. Many fathers—some I've seen coach my own kids—would have called their son "stupid" for owning up to what Matthew did, not courageous. But not my friend.

> COURAGE TO DO THE RIGHT THING, WHICH
> IS AN IMPORTANT PART OF A HOME OF
> LIGHT, IS CULTIVATED WHEN
> PARENTS AFFIRM RIGHT CHOICES.

"Way to go, Matthew!" he said, and he meant it. The other team went on to score and ended up winning a close game. It was a costly lesson in doing what is right, but Matthew's father chose to affirm his son's decision as courageous.

Why is it so important to affirm such acts? Fast forward 20 years, and I'd want someone with Matthew's courage and integrity to make the hard decisions if he were operating on me, or representing me in negotiations, or leading our country, or pastoring a church, or being the kind of person one of our daughters might marry.

Courage to do the right thing, which is an important part of a home full of stability and faith, is cultivated when parents affirm right choices. Even if it's something as simple as writing a poem.

Looking Around You to Praise Small Acts of Courage

A few days after the World Trade Center fell, Cindy and I witnessed our daughter Laura do something courageous. It began early on the morning of September 11 as our family of four watched in horror as the first tower, and then the second, came crashing down.

Laura was only in fifth grade. She couldn't rush into the Twin Towers the way the heroic New York City firefighters did, or try to help others in the manner of the Port Authority and those brave police officers. Instead, Laura sat down later that day in her room and thought and prayed and cried for all the lives lost. Then she wrote a poem she titled "Now, More Than Ever." We had talked about this theme during the day, but the following words (and spelling and grammar) are all her own:

Now More Than Ever...

Now more than ever we need to stand strong,
Now more than ever we need to be one,
Now more than ever we need to fight back,
To prove what is right, to prove we are strong
Now more than ever we need to hold on,
To keep our country together
And our flag waving long,
Now more than ever we need to have friends.
Families will struggle but will win in the end,
Now more than ever we need our God,
He'll help us with pain and He'll help us with life.
Let's stand up and help each other
Through this struggle of faith
Let us never forget the tears that we've shed
Of those who are lost and those who are dead
Now more than ever we need to stand strong,
To fight all the evil, Lord please keep us strong.

I realize it's the poem of an 11-year-old, not Tennyson. But it took courage for Laura to share her poem at the dinner table that night. It took courage for her to turn it in to her teacher the next day at school and to listen to some of her classmates snicker when her teacher asked her to read it to the class. Whether you're 11 or 81, it takes courage to write down your feelings and lay them before others. We praised Laura for her conviction to share what she felt God had put in her heart.

Three days later on Friday night, I saw another example of childlike courage in Kari, our older daughter. After much debate by the local school boards, the high school football games went on as scheduled in Arizona. That meant that Kari, a sophomore cheerleader on the varsity squad, would be cheering on the Eagles.

This was the first football game of the season, and the first game Cindy and I would get to see the new cheer squad in action. The year before, Kari, along with five other freshmen and one sophomore, had surprised themselves and everyone by winning the Arizona State Cheerleading competition for small schools! When tryouts were held for the next year's squad, almost 40 girls came out.

A dozen girls made the varsity squad, and as we watched them perform that Friday night after September 11, my heart filled with pride and my eyes misted with tears. I wasn't choked up because of the emotion of the night, but because my heart was touched by the courage shown by Kari and her cheerleader friends—particularly the last cheerleader selected.

Her name is Brooke, a senior at Kari's school that year. Brooke is confined to an electric wheelchair because of cerebral palsy. She had always wanted to be a cheerleader. She has the smile and the enthusiasm to match any of the girls at school. But you can only dream of being a cheerleader if you can't walk, much less do the jumps and stunts. That is, unless the entire cheer squad and their coaches, Mrs. Lester and Miss Dalia, vote you onto the team. It was a dream come true for this inspirational young lady and a tremendous blessing for each girl and all the fans that night.

Picture two rows of cheerleaders in their sharp white outfits laced with red and blue, their school colors. Kari stood next to Brooke in the front row, and you could tell she was proud to be next to her friend.

When the girls turned to face the field with their hands on hips during the game, Brooke moved the toggle on her motorized wheelchair to face the field with them. When they turned back toward the crowd, Brooke turned with them as well. When they did a chant or cheer, Brooke was right there with them. With her eyes and voice and heart, she was every bit a member of the squad.

I know there was a football game going on that night, but my eyes were more frequently drawn to the sidelines where the cheerleaders performed. I was staggered by the courage Brooke showed in struggling to do each cheer the best she could. I was touched by the way Kari would pick up Brooke's pom-poms when she dropped them or make sure Brooke got a drink of water during timeouts. (It's still *hot* in Phoenix on September evenings.) And I was so proud of each and every girl on the cheer squad—Nicole and Kellee and

Laura and Lauren and Briana and Becca and Kourtney and Ashley and Sarah and Alexandra and Corrie—who loved Brooke as much as Kari. They, too, came over to encourage Brooke, get her drinks, and tell her she was doing a great job.

HONORING COURAGEOUS CHILDREN LIGHTS
UP THEIR LIVES AND OUR HOMES.

To put things in perspective, I attended the Rose Bowl in 1998 when my team, Arizona State, lost to Ohio State in the last 48 seconds of the game. I wasn't moved to tears then. I didn't even remember crying when I was a high school football player and we lost the city championship on a cold November night. But watching Kari and Brooke and the rest of the squad that evening, I kept choking up. I saw courage in ordinary kids doing something extraordinary—which is what our country will need in the stressful days ahead.

Whom in Your Community Can You Affirm?

Sure, these little stories of courage didn't win Congressional medals for Matthew, Laura, or Kari, and they aren't as dramatic as beating a drum and playing the fife to scare away British soldiers. But it took courage for Matthew to tell the truth, for Laura to share her thoughts in a heartfelt poem, and for Kari and a team of cheerleaders to reach out and see a classmate for what she could do, not for what she couldn't.

So the next time your children make a courageous choice, pin a medal on them by pointing their actions out to them and to others, if it's appropriate. Reinforce their virtue, values, resolve, faith, and character.

Honoring courageous children lights up their lives and our homes.

For now, more than ever, our country needs courageous kids who come from strong families.

Making Your Family Stronger

"Catching your kids doing something right" is a key to living out the fifth picture of a strong family. But just how do you spot acts of everyday courage? It's easy. Just set up a "courage detector" in your home.

You've already got a smoke detector. (Or you should.) You may well have a carbon monoxide detector or other type of alarm system. What I'm suggesting is that you set up a courage detector that measures ten types of courageous acts I will list below. That means that anytime you see one of your children doing one of these ten things, there's an automatic, "Way to go!" "I'm proud of you!" "Great choice!" "You have an awesome heart." "Do you know how special you are?" "You're making such wise decisions." "What you did shows so much character." "There's lots of adults who don't make the wise decisions you make." "With that kind of decision, you're going to do great when you grow up..." and so on.

Enlist your spouse and even brothers and sisters into being "courage detectors." For example, set out a small bell at the dinner table. Anytime during dinner, someone can pick up and ring that bell if they've seen their child or their sibling doing something from our list of ten things. I'll give you examples of three of the ten things that set off the detector, indicating everyday acts of courage lived out by your child. Then I'll provide the remaining seven that should make a connection and set off words of praise as well.

1. When your child doesn't hide a mistake, cover over something he accidentally broke, or otherwise chooses not to "cover up" something he's done wrong—the bell should go off.

Do you know what's at the heart of having integrity? In ancient Greek culture, unscrupulous vendors would take clay pots that emerged from the kiln with cracks and fill in the cracks with wax. These crooks would then paint the pots—hiding the problems—and sell them to unsuspecting customers. Can you picture what happened the first time one of those customers put hot liquid into the new pot he just purchased? It would be shown to have no integrity—for things (or people) with "integrity" are those things "without wax."

Share that story with your children, and then praise them when they have the courage to face up to a failing or mistake they've made. You'll be encouraging them to do something most people don't have the courage to do—be people who don't try to cover up cracks that, one day, everyone will see.

2. When they choose to do something right, especially when it's the more difficult choice or way—the bell should go off.

"Clean your room" can mean for some kids, "There's got to be more room under the bed or in the closet to cram all this stuff!" Anytime you see your children doing something the right way—particularly if what they've chosen to do takes longer or is more difficult, your "courage detector" should go off. For example, if you see them folding and hanging up their clean clothes, that's a more difficult path or choice than just throwing them in a drawer. Or if you see them set the egg timer for five *more* minutes of practice on the piano—or finish the selection they're playing *after* the timer went off—your "courage detector" should go off. In a world full of people looking for every shortcut—and sacrificing excellence as a result—choosing to do something the right way, even if it's the hard way, should draw praise for that act of courage.

3. When your child could "gossip" about another child, but doesn't, or chooses not to join in a taunting session with a weaker or vulnerable child—the bell should go off.

Here's another way to spot and praise courage in children. Anytime you see them showing compassion or having the character to walk away from a gossip session, you should sound the positive courage bell. By the way, do you know what it literally means to slander another person? It means to "spy" on them. Meaning, what a "spy" does is get close to someone and then use that information to harm them. We slander someone when we use insider info to destroy their person or character. When your child chooses not to be a hurtful spy, but a person of character—that takes courage, and such courage should be affirmed.

Where do you find the remaining seven examples of things that should set off the bell in your home? From Psalm 15, where I drew these three examples. Here's the Trent translation of this powerful psalm, with ten traits of a person of godly character—each of which should be tied into your "courage detector."

Psalm 15
A Psalm of David the King

O Lord, who may be Your traveling companion on earth,

And dwell forever with You in Heaven?

   [The answer? In our personal life...]

It's someone who walks without wax in seamless integrity [trait 1],

Trusts You for the power to do what's right (even when it's the difficult way) [trait 2],

And strives to tell himself and others the truth, even if it hurts [trait 3].

   [In our important relationships...]

It's someone who doesn't gather "inside information," like a "spy," on a friend and then twist or use it with others to harm them [trait 4],

He or she avoids choices that he knows will harm his neighbor [trait 5],

And refuses to carry a grudge against a good friend [trait 6].

   [And in our dealings with everyone...]

It's someone who rejects those who are and do evil, but
   honors those who walk close to the Lord [trait 7],
They're the kind of person who makes a commitment
   as strong as a "seven-strand rope" and doesn't look
   for a way to "barter" their way out [trait 8],
They don't lend money to those in need at loan-shark
   rates [trait 9],
Nor do they put gaining money over treating people
   well and having integrity [trait 10],
[And there's a promise from God for those who live
   such a life…]
He who does these things will never be shaken.

The Sixth Picture

RECONCILING RELATIONSHIPS

I'm a veteran of exactly one marathon. Running 26.2 miles at the 2001 Rock 'n' Roll Marathon in San Diego was a major achievement for me. The colorful medal I received for finishing the race hangs proudly on the edge of a file cabinet next to my desk. But don't ask me what my time was, although I can give you a hint: I came in just *behind* the lady pushing the jogging stroller. Put another way, the men's winner barely nipped me, crossing the finish line a mere two-and-a-half hours ahead of my time.

I found out firsthand that with each mile, a marathon becomes more challenging. As the distance increases, so do the extra sweatshirts and fanny packs tossed by runners to the side of the road. Extra ounces can feel like extra pounds by the 20-mile mark.

But what if you had to run that kind of endurance race wearing five-pound ankle weights? That wouldn't be a handicap in a marathon—that would be punishment. With ankle weights, it wouldn't take long before each mile—each step—would become agony.

Finishing such a long race would be impossible for all but a few.

"But no one runs marathons with ankle weights!" you might say. I disagree. In fact, I see people arrive every week in my counseling office wearing heavy ankle weights. Some are carrying five, ten, even twenty pounds of emotional weight they've had for years. It doesn't stop them from walking, but it certainly holds them back from "running a good race," as the apostle Paul calls it (Galatians 5:7 NIV). What's more, those ankle weights are the very things that prevent many people from reaching the goal of having a strong family.

These emotional leg weights, for the most part, are past hurts strapped on tightly by an unwillingness to reconcile relationships. For example, perhaps you left your parents' home in anger as a teenager, and you never closed the loop or made things right with Mom or Dad. That's a ten-pound weight you carry to every family event you go to, especially during the long holiday season.

Another example would be having a long-term relationship break apart and still, years later, be carrying around hatred for the other person. (Not "intense dislike," but acid-dipped hatred.) Hating an ex-spouse can easily be a 20-pound weight—one that we carry, not them—even if they were the one who walked away from the marriage or hurt the children. Then there are those who suffer a financial setback or are cheated by another person (or both) and make a decision to despise the one who hurt them. That degree of daily anger can drag down one's ability to enjoy life or build solid relationships.

Using a different metaphor, the apostle John pictures the problem of hating others as causing us to lose direction, focus, and purpose. "The one who says he is in the Light and yet hates his brother is in the darkness until now....But the one who hates his brother is in the darkness and walks in the darkness, and does not know where he is going because the darkness has blinded his eyes" (1 John 2:9,11).

If we're serious about having strong families, we must be free to move forward in life. In the "first picture," we saw how important it is to face up to and move on from past mistakes in our family. However, for many people, it's the emotional weights with others, not just immediate family, that cause us to stumble and rob us of the light. Thankfully, there's a "new" word that can help us.

Something "New" to Help Move Your Life Forward

"Learning to Forgive Can Benefit the Forgiver" ran a bold headline from an article in *USA Today* (August 28, 2001). In a study of 259 adults reported by Stanford University psychologist Dr. Carl Thoresen at an annual meeting of the American Psychological Association, those who learned to forgive others saw "stress, anger and psychosomatic symptoms—headaches, stomach upsets, etc.—go way down, significantly lower than for the control group." Likewise, Case Western psychologist Julie Exline concurred, discovering that just writing about a painful incident (for example, writing a letter but never sending it) can "dispel bad feelings."

Isn't it amazing how the "mounting evidence" confirms what the Bible has told us all along: We gain life, freedom, and direction when we forgive, and we gain stronger families and homes of far brighter light as well.

Dr. Thoresen's study also noted: "A forgiving nature may also improve intimate relationships. Compared with people reluctant to forgive, the forgivers saw romantic partners in a more positive light and reported a more loving relationship."

Translation: Strong marriages and families are inhabited by people who don't explain away or minimize wrong, but who get rid of the ankle weights of hate or bitterness as best they can and as quickly as possible.

It's worth recalling that the Greek word for "forgiveness" means to "untie the knot." That's why I used the image of ankle weights laced up tight to describe a person who refuses to forgive or deal with past relationships. The more weighed down we are, the less we're free to run alongside each other in this thing called life.

I saw that in my relationship with my father.

Leaving Behind My Ankle Weights

For years I hated him. I absolutely hated my father. He left my mother and us three boys when I was only two months old. I never met the man until my teen years, even though we all lived in the Phoenix area. Even then, he did little to build a relationship with us, and he never once brought up the subject of why he left Mom, nor did he ever say he was sorry.

Then I became a Christian while I was in high school. I'd like to say that on that very night I unshackled my ankle weights of hate for my father, but that wasn't true. Instead of hating him, I just "intensely disliked" him. It took many years—until I was almost through college—before I finally faced the fact that I was the one weighted down by my anger, not him. I was the one losing sleep and quality of life as each mile of life passed by, not him.

WITH GOD'S HELP, WE CAN RELEASE OUR GRIP ON THE PICTURES THAT HAVE STAYED WITH US FOR SO LONG, EVEN THE PAINFUL ONES.

I purposely called Dad and asked him to meet me at a nearby Red Lobster in Phoenix. When the main course arrived, I got to the main reason I invited him out to dinner. I wanted to ask his forgiveness for being so angry with him all those years.

I didn't ask Dad to explain away his behavior in leaving. I didn't demand that he explain why he still chose to stay out of his sons' lives—and the lives of his grandchildren. I didn't ask for an apology, nor did I expect to receive one, which is good, because he didn't speak any words of regret.

I'm not sure what happened in my father's heart that night when we walked away from the table, but I know what happened in mine. Whoever cleared away our table also found the pair of ankle weights I left behind.

After that Red Lobster dinner, I began to look at my father in a different way. Remember how the apostle John says you walk out of darkness when you forgive, but you can't see because of the darkness when you don't? Once I forgave my father, I began to actually notice how lonely he was. While he wouldn't talk about his background, I learned later from my Uncle Max how much my father had suffered both as a child and as a soldier fighting in the Pacific during World War II. Without making excuses for what he did or didn't do, I finally could see something of the struggle he'd had. I was able to feel compassion for him.

I wish there were a storybook ending to this story. Unfortunately, my father died without even knowing the name of my youngest daughter. But on his last day on earth, I was there for him at the hospice on the corner of Tatum and Paradise Village Parkway. I held his hand for eight and a half hours, prayed for him, and was able to love him because I'd forgiven him—and most of all because I'd been forgiven by a loving God.

With God's help, we can release our grip on the pictures that have stayed with us for so long, even the painful, hurtful ones. We can forgive and be forgiven, replacing the bad memories of the past with images of love and hope and beauty.

Which brings me to the question I'm sure you saw coming at the start of this chapter. Is there a relationship you need to reconcile?

Is there a past relationship with a spouse, a former business partner, or even with God that needs to be dealt with?

Are there ankle weights you need to take off—perhaps today?

For now, more than ever, we need to reconcile relationships if our home is to be a place lit up by God's love.

❦

Making Your Family Stronger

We're challenged in this chapter not just to take responsibility for our own actions and "untie the knots," but to face up to the ways other people have hurt us, even to extending forgiveness. That's a challenge to live out, particularly if you come from one of the following "hard to leave" homes. Take time with your spouse, friend, or small group to read and talk through the following examples. Do you see any of these issues still unresolved in your life and past? In the lives of loved ones or friends?

A "hard to leave" home is a home that specializes in making the journey to healthy independence steeper and more rocky. To move out emotionally from a "hard to leave" home takes extra effort and often an extra reliance on God's strength and wisdom. That's especially true if you come from one (or more) of the three most common "hard to leave" homes I see in counseling.

1. Homes That Erase Our Identity

Anna grew up in a home where her parents couldn't see eye to eye on anything. Unfortunately, her mother compensated for an unfulfilling marriage by making her only daughter, Anna, the focus of her time, energy, and attention. All that attention may have been positive at first, but at some point it crossed the line into smothering. She was so involved and so possessive that Anna soon found her identity only in her mother. Then Anna started grade school.

An observant teacher noticed how much Anna was struggling with relating to other children and called in the school psychologist.

"Anna," he said, "Would you please draw a picture of everyone in your family?"

Quickly she drew a picture of herself standing next to her mother, with her father and brothers at a distance.

"Now, I'd like for you to draw a picture of everyone in your home except you." When Anna turned in the picture this time, there was only her father and two brothers.

"I'm sorry," he commented. "Let me explain again what I'd like for you to do. I'd like you to draw a picture of everyone in your family, *except you*. Just leave yourself out and put everyone else in the picture."

A second time the picture came back with Anna—and her mother—left out. Can you begin to see what was happening with this young child? To leave out herself meant to leave out her mother. There was simply no "self" apart from her overinvolved mother. Fast-forward a number of years and think of how high the bar gets set when Anna tries to "connect" with her husband—and let her mother remain with the rest of her family.

We are all wonderfully and uniquely made to reflect God's image and are not intended to be shadows of someone else, even if that someone is a beloved parent. It's wonderful to love our parents with our whole hearts, but growing up without an independent identity can create a "hard to leave" home and the need to reconcile a relationship.

2. Homes That Shine an Unhealthy Spotlight

For Bill, the first child—and the first grandchild—in the family, growing up meant six years of having a single spotlight of love and attention. Again, there's nothing wrong with affection, caring, and closeness. But in Bill's home, all that attention, combined with no discipline and lavish expenditures on toys, clothes and, later, cars, left a deep seated self-centeredness. Take an unwillingness, or lack of knowing how, to share the spotlight with a spouse and watch the problems mount. His birthday is a big deal. Her birthday receives one-tenth the attention. His accomplishments are what's important. Her promotion barely draws a comment.

An environment that pushes us out of balance when it comes to serving, praising, or being sensitive to others' needs can create a "hard to leave" home and set up hurdles to closeness that must come down.

3. Homes Where Boundaries Don't Exist

Perhaps the most difficult of all "hard to leave" homes comes when there weren't "protective fences" in the home. Clinical studies show that grade school children use more of a playground area and exhibit less aggressive play when there's a fence around the playground. Now think about that in relation to a home. When we grow up within a protected area, we're freer to learn and grow and carry far less anger. When we grow up where boundaries were violated, that environment can leave long-lasting hurt and anger. Which is where we need God's help and strength in knowing two things. First, we benefit when we "untie the knots" and forgive another person; and second, ultimately, a righteous God administers justice, meaning we don't have to be in the revenge business.

Having read through these three "hard to leave" homes, do you have a fourth that comes to mind as you think about reconciling past relationships? Whatever the situation, we gain ground in our family when we "close the loop" and move forward.

The Seventh Picture

VALUING AND LISTENING TO OUR SENIORS

*I*t's another enduring memory from my childhood. I'm perched up in "my tree" in our front yard, high atop one of three grapefruit trees—one for each boy in the family. My older brother, Joe, had his own tree that was strictly off-limits to anyone else. His tree was located on the east side of the yard, nearest the lamp post. Jeff, my twin brother, had "dibs" on the tree closest to the carport on the west side of the yard. That left "my tree," which was smack dab in the middle of the yard.

As I peek through the branches and look toward the house, I can see inside the bay window. There's my grandfather, sitting in his favorite chair at our old kitchen table. I think I'm hidden, but his sharp gray eyes see me looking at him. He smiles and lifts up his coffee cup in salute with those big, rough carpenter's hands of his.

I wish now I'd taken that smile as an invitation. I wish I would have climbed out of my tree and perched myself next to that tall Texan that day—the grandfather

I never really got to know. But there were so many important things to do when I was seven years old. I had backyard forts to defend and front yard trees to climb. I didn't know that in two months he would die of a brain aneurysm, and we would never have that talk.

I'm afraid I'm not alone in having missed opportunities to hear priceless stories about family history, or to gain wisdom from the trials an elder family member faced, or to just sit and let them know how much I love them by listening at length, without looking at my watch.

Too many members of the baby boom generation—and now their grown-up children—are letting parents and grandparents and aunts and uncles slip into eternity without ever once having those long talks. Often it's because we're too busy climbing the corporate ladder or tackling another home improvement project—and I can relate.

HE SMILES AND LIFTS UP HIS COFFEE CUP
IN SALUTE WITH THOSE BIG, ROUGH
CARPENTER'S HANDS OF HIS.

I know how time-starved we all are, and I also know that making time for long talks with older family members is asking a great deal. But take it from me, someone who is in his fifties but who has already buried his parents, grandparents, and all but one uncle and aunt: There's an even greater sense of loss when they're no longer around to talk to.

If you're serious about having strong families and homes full of light and are still blessed with living next of kin, there's no better time than now to set aside some hours in your busy schedule for long talks with your seniors. That's something my friend Darryl did recently, and that decision to reach out to a close relative is still impacting both their lives.

Marching Back Through Time

A tremendously popular HBO program that debuted during 2001 was *Band of Brothers,* based on a book by Stephen Ambrose. Ambrose's story and the HBO series by the same name follow a company of airborne rangers (Charlie Company, 501st Airborne) from the time they jumped into Normandy on D day until the end of the war outside Berlin.

On a flight from Michigan to Phoenix, I sat next to my good friend, Darryl, who told me about a special trip he'd just made to see his favorite uncle, who happened to be in poor health. Darryl's Uncle Jim had fought with his own "band of brothers" as a member of the 527th Airborne from D day to VE (Victory in Europe) day.

Darryl shared that he'd picked up a car at the airport and driven several hours to his uncle's home. Following a warm greeting, the first thing Uncle Jim did was bring out his wedding pictures. Standing in those faded photographs was a four-year-old boy— Darryl! The photos were taken during the early days of World War II when Darryl was the ring bearer in his uncle's wedding. One picture showed the smiling four-year-old dressed in a military uniform tailored just for him, marching down the aisle of the church. Then, shortly after Uncle Jim said, "I do," he marched off to the European theater.

Uncle Jim was a card-carrying member of "The Greatest Generation," a war hero who parachuted into Holland, participated in the liberation of France, backtracked to save American forces trapped in the Battle of the Bulge, fought his way across the Rhine, and lived to make it to Berlin. That day he talked to Darryl about everything, from the wedding photos to family history questions. How he first met his wife. What he did before the war and immediately afterward. And then, as the conversation warmed, Darryl asked his uncle what it was like being a paratrooper during the greatest military campaign of the twentieth century.

Uncle Jim was quiet for a long moment. Finally, he breathed deeply, stood up, and walked to a back room. He returned several minutes later with an old, creased shoe box. Slowly, he took off the lid, revealing a jumble of decorations for valor from France and Belgium, a Silver Star, and his Purple Heart. Each ribbon had a story. Each story brought back a flood of memories. And each memory brought to the surface longsuppressed feelings his uncle had pushed to the back of his mind.

Tears flowed that afternoon—both from Uncle Jim and from Darryl. Tears as Uncle Jim shared about the horrible sight of being the first one to reach a glider full of dead men the day after D day. Of the terrible hedgerows by day and the horrors of artillery shells at night. Of gunmetal being so cold at Bastogne that it would rip the skin off your hands. Of watching your best friend take a sniper's bullet in the neck as he stood only three feet from you—and having him die in your arms three weeks before the war was over.

Afternoon turned to evening, and they made sandwiches and soup. All that time the stories continued. Finally, it was time for Darryl to drive the three hours back to where he'd spend the night and then hook up with me for the flight home to Phoenix.

But Darryl's uncle wanted to share two last things with him…his box and his thanks.

"It's for you," said Uncle Jim, as he handed over his box. "I'm real sick, Darryl, you know that. And I'd like you to have these. I think they'd mean something to you."

Darryl protested. Such priceless pictures of heroism and sacrifice should go to his children, not a nephew. But Uncle Jim insisted, forcing the old shoe box under his arm.

"You're the only one who's ever asked," Uncle Jim said.

"What do you mean?"

"None of my children have ever sat down with me like this," he replied. "Not one of the three ever asked about what happened to me before the war, or during the war, like you. Thank you for asking."

Go Sit at the Kitchen Table if You Can

I'm back, sitting in my tree…peeking through the leaves at my grandfather sitting at the kitchen table. Forty-two years later, I wish I'd been wise enough to go inside and have a long talk with him. I can actually remember feeling a pang of guilt back then, but that impulse was interrupted when I had to repel invaders (my two brothers) from trying to climb my tree.

I thought there would always be time to sit at the kitchen table and talk with Grandfather. You know, someday when the weather wasn't so nice. Then came St. Patrick's day, just a few weeks later. That day etched another memory, but one much more sorrowful. That was the day my grandfather passed away suddenly inside the house while we kids were playing outside.

In Hebrews 3:7-8 there's a strong admonition not to wait when it comes to seeking out God. "Today, if you hear his voice, do not harden your heart" (NIV). That's because we may only have today to respond.

By application, I feel a similar focus on "today" is crucial in our personal relationships—and especially with our seniors.

Today, if you're serious about having a strong family, don't overlook the seniors in your life. Parents and aunts and uncles may want to share their hearts with you as much as you want to hear from them. You can also seek out older friends in your neighborhood or church because they have much to share as well—not just stories, but wisdom and love and insight into others. People in past generations occupied their minds less with technology and more with people. You may be surprised at the wonderful insights they can't wait to share.

But that means climbing down from your perch in the tree and sitting at the kitchen table. My grandfather's death taught me a valuable lesson—one that helped me during my teen years. I made a point then to sit down with my grandmother and have a number of "long talks." I learned so much about the Thomasons and

Harts and Trimbles and other assorted relatives in Indiana, and what it was like for her to grow up on a farm, to get married at 16, and to move from Kansas to Texas in a covered wagon.

I remembered that lesson of having long talks even in the midst of raising young children and building a career—long talks with Cindy and long talks with my mother. And now that my mother has passed away, I've *never* regretted one moment sitting at her kitchen table.

Isn't it time you sat down with a close family member or older loved one? It may be later than you think, for now, more than ever, we need to have long talks with our seniors.

Making Your Family Stronger

There is a well-known tourist attraction in Tucson, Arizona, that draws movie buffs by the thousands each year. It's called "Old Tucson," and it's a Western town where literally hundreds of movies have been shot. Walk the streets of that town and you'll find the Livery Stable, the Mercantile, the Bank (which is robbed every evening at 5:00), and, of course, the Jail (for the few stunt men who weren't gunned down by the Sheriff).

But there's one small problem with this Western "city." It's all facades. It's row after row of buildings with only their fronts facing the street. And that's just what many of us face when it comes to our seniors.

As you seek to reach out to older loved ones, be honest. Is your relationship with that person like dealing with a facade? Cordial. Friendly. A weather-report relationship that never goes any deeper. Or is there depth and substance to your relationship with your senior? Have you ever walked through the door and looked inside?

I can remember packing every square inch of my car the day I headed off to Texas for college from our home in Phoenix. I also remember driving back home five minutes after I'd finally left because I'd forgotten my sunglasses. (In Arizona, it soon becomes very clear when you've forgotten your sunglasses!)

What I didn't expect was walking back in the door and seeing my precious mother sitting at our old kitchen table, crying. I was the last to leave the nest, and now we hugged and cried and sat down and talked a little more before I finally left.

Which leads me to something I do, and encourage you to do, to build a better, stronger, less facade-oriented relationship with your senior.

Forget your sunglasses on purpose.

Don't be in such a hurry to leave that you can't turn around unexpectedly, sit down, take a little more time, ask a few more questions, and tell them one more time you love and appreciate them. That may be the best thing you ever "forget" to do.

The Eighth Picture

REMEMBERING TO SMILE

*J*t was December 24, 1944. Christmas that year was a tough time for our country, especially for one young Marine sitting stiffly in an overcrowded train. This was day two of four days and four nights that Corporal Edward Andrusko would spend traveling by train from San Diego to New York. Each passenger car was packed with sailors, soldiers, and Marines trying to get home for Christmas.

Already they had traveled through bleak deserts, a blizzard in Denver, and what seemed like endless frozen prairies and farmland. The whole trip inched by under unrelenting gray clouds, but time didn't seem to matter. Nothing seemed to matter. Recovering from his third wound received in battle and a painful case of malaria, Corporal Andrusko would arrive home in New York the day after Christmas. Even that seemed fitting.

"I would miss Christmas at home by a day," he wrote afterward. *"My parents had split up, and I had no home to go to. My girlfriend of four years sent me a Dear John*

letter, saying she had waited too long for me to return and found someone else. And worst of all, when I was well enough for duty, I could be sent overseas to battle again."[6]

Darkness had fallen, and the train had stopped at a small, dimly lit railroad station about two hours outside Chicago. Large snowdrifts blocked any view from the train. In that cold, dark tunnel of a station, peace and light and love—even thoughts of a loving God—seemed nonexistent.

Earlier in the evening, Andrusko had spoken with a fellow Marine nicknamed "Ski" who was returning home minus his right arm. *"Ski and I agreed that we both became near atheists and cynics after three years of war,"*[7] he remembers. But for one Marine at least, all that would change with a smile.

"It Came Upon a Midnight Clear…"

Few men were awake as the train sat at the station, but Andrusko's war wound and the malaria his body fought made sleep a challenge—particularly having to sleep sitting up the entire trip. It was at that dark moment in his young life that the door at the other end of the train car opened.

From Andrusko's seat far in the back, he could barely see a small boy and an elderly lady enter the car. He lost sight of them altogether as they walked slowly down the aisle. Apparently they were looking for a seat. Andrusko closed his eyes and tried to go back to sleep, but a noise near him caused him to open his eyes. Standing right in front of him was the young boy and the lady.

"Welcome home and Merry Christmas, Marine." The young boy smiled as he extended his little hand.

"My grandmother and I would like to give you a gift and thank you for serving our country." The little boy shook the wounded Marine's hand and handed him a crumpled one dollar bill. His grandmother put her arm around him and said, "God bless you." And then they both smiled and said, "Merry Christmas, and goodbye."

Andrusko tried to grab his sea bag from under the seat to try to find a candy bar or some kind of gift he could give them, but when he looked up, they were gone—so quickly that he wondered if what had just happened was real or a dream. Later, he asked Ski and two soldiers seated nearby if they'd seen the young boy and his grandmother come onto the train. No one had. They told him he was dreaming. Yet there in his hand was the crumpled one-dollar bill.

With that smile and small gift, *"I contentedly fell asleep with my precious gift tucked safely in my pocket,"* he recounted, *"and a pleasant feeling in my heart, the nicest feeling I had had in a very long time."*[8]

Corporal Andrusko credits that night with changing his bitter feelings after the war. But in his mind, it took another child, many years later, to explain to him why that was true.

More than 50 years passed, and the Marine on the train was now as old as the grandmother he'd met that night. It was Christmastime again, and Corporal Andrusko was surrounded by his family gathered for a Christmas celebration, not a train full of weary soldiers. During a lull in the activity, he recounted to everyone the story of the little boy on the train. It was the reminiscing of a soldier grown old. As he finished, Andrusko asked a question, really to no one in particular: "Who was that little boy on the train, and why did he and his grandmother choose me? Why me?"

A young niece was visiting, and she had listened to her uncle's wartime story and his unanswered questions. "I know," she said quietly.

Everyone stopped to look at her.

The old Marine said, "You know what?"

"I know who the little boy on the train was, and why he picked you." She paused, very deliberately, and then said,

"The little boy was God, and he chose you because you were very, very sad and disappointed with everyone and everything. He wanted to make you happy again and welcome you home—and he did."[9]

Out of the mouth of another child came words of healing and light—and a smile. You can argue the point theologically, but you'll never convince an old Marine and a young child that God didn't show up in that train, wrapped in the warm smile of a young boy.

And God's love still shows up today on the smiling faces of children and adults.

A Smile Can Light Up the Darkness

Smiles and laughter didn't end on a blood-soaked Pacific island for a wounded Marine, nor did they die in the burial ground the World Trade Center became on September 11. Certainly then our hearts were robbed of mirth and eyes filled with tears. But in words of the psalmist, "Weeping may last for the night, but a shout of joy comes in the morning" (Psalm 30:5). That's because we are people with hope. Again the psalmist encourages us with the words, "Light arises in the darkness for the upright" (Psalm 112:4).

Even for those who are hurting, laughter can help lift their load. Put in biblical terms, "Bright eyes gladden the heart; good news puts fat on the bones," says Proverbs 15:30. As difficult a time as our nation faces today, one of the great American character traits we possess is our faith in God that gives us the ability to smile, to joke, and even to laugh at ourselves in difficult times.

Laughter and smiles are signs of strength of character, not of weakness. Returning again to the psalmist, we read: "Then our mouth was filled with laughter and our tongue with joyful shouting; then they said among the nations, 'The LORD has done great things for them'" (Psalm 126:2). Our joy can be a witness to the world of our hope that lies within.

Smiles Are Good Medicine for the Heart

There is an old Norwegian proverb that says, "He who laughs, lasts." Numerous clinical studies show that laughter increases blood flow, lowers blood pressure, increases endorphin levels, and even decreases occurrences of second heart attacks. In short, medical science keeps proving what the Bible noted hundreds of years ago. "A joyful heart is good medicine" (Proverbs 17:22).

Certainly, there are things in life that can rob us of our smile—if we let them. For example, I remember when my mother first began to struggle with rheumatoid arthritis. Over the course of several years, I watched her go from hiking desert hills to struggling to get down the hall with a cane. The arthritis forced her to retire from a job she loved and lose the ability to open jars or pick up grandchildren. But she never lost her smile. As she lay dying in a hospice near our home, one of her nurses told me, "John, I know your mother's hurting, but she glows whenever I come in."

LAUGHTER AND SMILES ARE SIGNS OF STRENGTH OF CHARACTER, NOT OF WEAKNESS.

Tragedy and trial are not laughing matters. But it's still healthy to laugh…and to smile…even at strangers. For you never know whose day you'll make.

One Last Look at a Great Crowd Full of Smiles

On the night when Corporal Andrusko met the little boy and his grandmother, he tells how the train pulled into Chicago's main train station around midnight. As he looked out the train window, hundreds of people of all ages and all races serenaded the soldiers with Christmas carols and passed out trays of food and drinks for them.

What a wonderful picture of the difference Christmas Day can make in the life of a wounded Marine…and in the life of a nation. Even in the midst of a war, the birth of the Christ child brings joy in the darkness—the Light of the world.

Making Your Family Stronger

How do you live out the encouragement that strengthens your family by "smiling" and adding laughter and joy to your home? For one thing, I'd urge you to go to the church of your choice. Not because you'll find a stand-up monologue each week, but because you will find out the truth of Psalm 16:11, which states that in the presence of the Lord is fullness of joy.

There is no greater joy than knowing we're forever loved, fully accepted, undeservedly forgiven, and that we get to spend eternity with the One who created us. Even in difficult times and when facing major challenges, knowing we're loved by the God who can make our home a place of greater warmth and love. And then here's another thing I'd suggest.

Be willing to take the lead in smiles in your home—even if it means sharing a "most embarrassing moment."

For example, when my daughters were young, there's a story they forced me to tell over and over to people who came to our home. During or after dinner with this new person, they'd say, "Tell them your 'Big Date' story, Dad! Tell them your 'Big Date' story." The chant would continue until I recounted the facts of that fateful day.

During my first semester in college, I had a roommate who worked at the local movie theater. It was a beautiful, huge theater, and because he owed me for lots of homework help, he presented me with two "manager's passes" to the original screening of *Star*

Wars. What this meant was that I didn't have to get to the theater hours ahead of time like the millions of other people who went to that movie. While people were wrapped around the building, I could walk right up to the very front of the line and be assured a great seat for the movie.

Those passes also meant I had a ticket to a Big Date.

With them in hand, I asked a young lady in one of my classes to go to see *Star Wars* with me. She was in the official "Beauty Queen" category as rated by each guy in my dorm, and amazingly, she said yes. (Meaning she hadn't seen the movie and, after I had explained about the manager's passes, she didn't want to wait in line.)

Sure, she was going to see the movie, not be with me, but all I cared about was that I had a date with the Beauty Queen! I kicked into full, "Get ready for my big date!" mode.

I washed my small pickup truck, got my hair cut, and even did the laundry. In particular, I wanted to be able to wear my new "super cool" bell-bottom pants. Because I'm really old, and because I had really bad taste in clothes back in the '70s, I actually wore those pants with the huge flared legs—and they were indeed a beautiful shade of light orange.

I could tell my date was impressed when I picked her up and she insisted on calling me "Jim." Not wanting to embarrass her, I didn't object, and soon we were at the theater. Moving to the front of an incredible line, we still had to wait for about 20 minutes before we were let in—and that's when it happened. As we stood in line outside the theater, I felt something brush up against my leg from the inside of my flared pants.

I smacked at whatever it was, thinking it was a bug, but it was no such luck. As I mentioned, I'd done my laundry earlier that day. Being a typical guy, I threw everything into the washing machine and then into the dryer without separating anything. The terrible thing that had happened was captured in two words—static cling. In the dryer, a pair of my underwear had somehow attached themselves inside the huge flair of my bell-bottoms! What I was feeling now was the static cling beginning to loosen and the underwear beginning to slide down my leg!

Finally, the underpants completed their descent and rested on my left shoe. Imagine my horror! Here I was, standing in line at a theater next to a beautiful girl, getting ready to watch an epic movie, and suddenly I have a pair of underwear on my left foot—and she was standing on my left side! As I tried nonchalantly to get her to change sides, the lady behind me suddenly utters a "Yuuukk!" really loud, and the guy with her says, "Hey, buddy, did you just lose your underwear?"

Needless to say, that was my one and only date with the Beauty Queen. The only good thing was that she went back to her dorm telling everyone about this dweeb named "Jim" with underwear on his shoe. But what I lost in pride that day, I gained in countless smiles ever since at the dinner table. Which brings me back to how to live out this eighth picture of a strong family.

Don't be afraid to laugh or share funny stories or let the kids share their funny jokes or stories at the table, family room, or halls of your home. The more laughter that bounces off the walls of your house when the children are growing up, the more smiles you'll carry on your face and heart when their rooms are empty and your family is just you and your spouse.

The Ninth Picture

OPENING OUR EYES TO A STRONG FAITH

ry on this plot for a modern-day thriller.

A nation of zealots decides to launch a clandestine war against its much larger neighbor. Knowing they'll be defeated in direct battle with their enemy, they instead plan a series of ambushes that will kill as many people as possible. Even though they can't win in open warfare, these special ops killings will give them victory after victory until the larger nation finally agrees to their demands.

Confident of their strategy, these killers pick several "high value" targets, carefully set their first big ambush, and then wait for the jaws of death to snap shut on those they hate. But when the day of death arrives, no one walks into the prearranged killing zone. No one!

The first time their deadly planning doesn't pay off, they attribute it to blind luck on behalf of their enemy. Patiently, methodically, another target is set. Another day of destruction is planned for those they hate, but the same thing happens—not a single target comes within range!

Now they know their secret operation has been compromised. They have no idea if the CIA, FBI, or NSA has hacked into their operation plans, but they're certain there's a problem. Most likely, it involves a traitorous mole.

They scour their headquarters, where someone finally finds a long-range listening device inside the commander in chief's personal office. No wonder their plans have been thwarted! Using their own intelligence, they track the device back to its source—a safe house where a known spymaster is living. This time, instead of sending killer squads, the furious leader orders hundreds of soldiers to surround the source of the leak in the middle of the night. They will eradicate him and his men in the morning, and then start planning their killing missions all over again.

Just minutes before they launch their attack at dawn, a lowly aide at the spy headquarters walks outside—and he sees the masses of deadly forces silently waiting. He runs back inside crying, "We're surrounded! We're all going to be killed!"

"Calm down," announces the spymaster, seemingly unruffled in the face of certain death. "We'll be fine. You just need to slip these on." In his hands are super high-tech laser-vision lenses attached to a headband. "Just look out the window," he says, handing over the special lenses.

Amazingly, with these goggles on, the aide can see what the terrorists can't. Namely, forming up behind them—invisible to those without the special lenses—are "black ops" helicopters bristling with armed soldiers.

With the laser-vision lenses he can see stealth fighters making their final turns, lining up their bomb and strafing runs. The terrorists are about to go from dangerous to deceased, and the aide goes from fear to faith—because his eyes were opened to a source of help and strength hidden from his sight.

Open the Eyes of Our Heart, Lord

A possible script from Stephen Spielberg? Not exactly. Try a modern-day version of a story right out of the Bible! The story I'm referring to took place at a time of war for the nation of Israel, and it does indeed hold great parallels and important truths for today.

The Bible shares in 2 Kings 6 how the king of Aram decided to set traps for the soldiers of Israel by sending men to camp out on known roads so that they could ambush and kill them. But time and again, the king's plans were thwarted.

The king of Aram was furious, and he finally found out that the "spy" was none other than the prophet Elisha, who was relaying information to the king of Israel and averting tragedy for Israel's soldiers.

Just as in the story above, the king of Aram was so furious (discovering you've been spied upon can do that to you) that he sent a host of troops to surround and kill Elisha. Sure enough, a servant of the great prophet went out early one morning and saw their imminent peril. That's when the very first "night vision" goggles were handed out by Elisha to his fearful servant. Not literal goggles, but "eyes of faith."

In that dark hour, with fear gripping his heart, Elisha prays for his servant: *"Do not fear, for those who are with us are more than those who are with them"* (2 Kings 6:16). That's something neither the aide in the imaginary story above nor Elisha's servant could see—until their eyes were opened.

Elisha continues his prayer for his fearful friend, asking Almighty God, *"'O LORD, I pray, open his eyes that he may see.'* And the LORD opened the servant's eyes and he saw; and behold, the mountain was full of horses and chariots of fire all around Elisha" (2 Kings 6:17).

The enemy of God's people wasn't victorious that day, nor will it be in our day. Particularly if we learn how to have "eyes of faith" in fearful times.

The Need for Strong Mentors, Leaders, and Communities of Faith

In these days full of WMD (weapons of mass destruction) scares and terrorist threats, it's easy to feel that we're surrounded by evil and darkness. Yet it is faith in spite of fear that opens our eyes to see beyond the darkness to the light beyond.

The writer of the book of Hebrews says this about faith: "Faith is the assurance of things hoped for, the conviction of things not seen" (Hebrews 11:1). Great faith in our day means living out a bold faith as well. It means being sure of our hope in a cause that's right before the victory over terror is finished. It means being certain that God cares for us, even when we shake our heads at another act of terror on our shores. It means being confident in the fact that a positive outcome not seen is still an outcome that's sure.

You'll notice as well that the servant of Elisha did at least one thing right in his fear—he ran to a person of strong faith. I submit that those of us who want to build strong families need to draw strength and courage from mentors and leaders who are people of great faith. Where do you find such people, who can be godly examples to you and your children? A great place to begin is your local church.

GREAT FAITH IN OUR DAY MEANS
LIVING OUT A BOLD FAITH AS WELL.

Whatever city or town you're in, take a look around at those whose lives you have seen changed by going to church—and then follow them Sunday morning or Saturday night.

Just follow a changed life, and you'll be following someone like Elisha's servant, who had his eyes opened. A person who may have been fearful and surrounded by the worst-case scenario, but someone who then found strength in a loving God.

For now, more than ever, we need to follow and become people of strong faith.

Making Your Family Stronger

There's a lot of "fuzzy thinking" out there.

For example, I just ran across a list of real-life quotes from corporate managers who were trying (and failing) to communicate important things to their subordinates. Here's an example of a "winning" memo:

As of tomorrow, employees will only be able to access the building using individual security cards. Pictures will be taken next Wednesday, and employees will receive their security cards in two weeks.

Or how about getting this memo from your boss:

What I need is an exact list of specific unknown problems we might encounter.

Or another winner:

This project is so important, we can't let things that are more important interfere with it.

Or my favorite:

We know that communication is a problem, but the company is not going to discuss it with the employees.

When it comes to having a strong family, there's no confusion about one thing—a strong faith is key to having a strong family in stressful times. Yet while it's easy to say, "I want to have a stronger faith," just what does that mean? After all, aren't we back to confusion over what it means to have faith?

Actually, the Bible defines faith for us in very clear terms. Hebrews 11:1 tells us that "Faith is the assurance of things hoped for, the conviction of things not seen."

While some may want to define faith as a "great leap" or "mystical state of mind," it's actually much more tangible than that. It's the kind of conviction that comes with knowing the sun will come up tomorrow.

It's the kind of assurance that good will come out of the situations we're in. And it's even the kind of belief that is leading balding people to sign up by the hundreds to hand over their hair for storage in an underground vault. Let me explain.

On April 28, 2002, an Associated Press story I read in the *Arizona Republic* told of a new company with booming profits and clients called Hairogenics. What they offer is to preserve several strands of your hair in their underground vault until the day scientists find a cure for baldness. When researchers come up with a way to create hair from the preserved DNA samples, people who have joined the program will be able to reverse their baldness with their own genetically grown hair!

Now that's "assurance in things hoped for" and "conviction of things not seen." Especially when it costs $49.95 for the hair sample kit and then $10.00 a month for storage!

Instead of basing their faith on the hopes of science, I'd suggest to those people that they base their faith on the unchanging God who loves them. They would also benefit by looking as a family at a great example of a strong faith.

That example is the life of Joseph in the Old Testament.

Start with his story in Genesis 37, and watch how many times this favored son (turned slave and then exalted ruler) believed in God's best, even in the darkest circumstances. Joseph had no assurance he would get out of the well his brothers threw him in, nor out of Pharaoh's prison when Potiphar's wife unjustly accused him, but he never lost hope in a positive future. In fact, talking again with the same brothers who had debated killing him, he tells them, "You meant evil against me, but God meant it for good in order to bring about this present result" (Genesis 50:20).

That's being able to see God's hand, by faith, even in the worst circumstances—and it's an essential trait to develop in your home. Take some time to look back over your life story. Divide your life into decades if you'd like, and list the high points and low points you've faced. From that view of your personal history, see if you can spot times when you exercised faith. When you believed, with full assurance, that something would happen—something that was out of your hands and out of your control.[10]

Teaching our children to put their hope and trust and faith in the Lord is all about helping them realize that God is indeed in control of things past, present, and in the future. May you know with more certainty than ever before that God is indeed a God worth trusting—a Savior worthy and deserving of our faith.

The Tenth Picture

BECOMING PEOPLE OF PRAYER

*I*n the *Los Angeles Times* magazine, writer Vince Rause and neuroscientist Andrew Newberg collaborated on an amazing article. It was titled, "Why God Won't Go Away," and it came to the "scientific" conclusion about something our whole country seems to remember in times of great trial. Namely, there is strong evidence that humans are "hardwired" to believe in God.

The natural need to turn to God in prayer has made a dramatic and public comeback since September 11. Just a sampling of headlines in the aftermath of the dark day read:

- "School, Local Govt's Turn to Prayer"

- "We're Letting God Back In"

- "ACLU Take Note: People Are Praying"

It's not just in the headlines, but in the hearts of Americans that prayer is making a comeback—and it should.

Prayer is like opening a window in a room that's unbearably hot. Prayer brings in the fresh air of hope and comfort. Prayer gives us courage, even as it provides an avenue for our hurt and pain to escape.

Prayer also gives us access to a loving God, even if we've been years in the asking. Just ask my Uncle Max.

A Long-Lost Relative Comes Home...

After graduating from high school, money was tight in our single-parent home, and so I stayed home for the first two years of college and saved a bundle on out-of-state tuition and room and board.

I receive a big break my junior year when I won a scholarship to attend Texas Christian University—known by many as TCU and home of the "Horned Frogs"—in Fort Worth, Texas. In my first semester, I received an assignment to write a paper in one class, but I was advised to do my research at the Southern Methodist University library in nearby Dallas. Sure, SMU was a big rival of TCU, but I was told that their library had voluminous amounts of material relating to my subject.

I walked into the SMU library lobby for the first time. To the right side of the circulation desk I noticed a glass-walled office. Upon closer inspection, I read a sign on the door announcing, "Robert M. Trent, Head Librarian."

Another Trent! Still, I knew the name "Trent" was common enough, so the chance of this Mr. Trent being blood kin was rather remote.

But never the shy type, I nonetheless decided to do something smart-alecky. I walked through the wide-open door and announced to the distinguished gentleman sitting at his desk, "Hi, Uncle Robert! I'm your long-lost nephew, John Trent, from Arizona."

I was just kidding, of course, thinking he'd laugh or explain that he didn't have any lost nephews.

Instead he looked at me intensely and asked, "Are you Joe Trent's boy?" My mouth fell open. I had no idea that I had an "Uncle Robert" in Texas. As we compared notes, I learned that he was my great-uncle— my father's uncle—but everyone called him by his middle name, Max.

Uncle Max graciously invited me to his home for dinner that night, where I met the love of his life for 45 years, Aunt Sally. She was a diminutive woman with piercing eyes and a wonderful sense of humor. They had never had any children, just each other, but they took a liking to me. I was soon adopted as a regular dinner guest.

One morning, Aunt Sally walked out to the driveway to pick up the hefty *Dallas Morning News* Sunday edition. As the same time, a tow truck driver—having overshot the address he was looking for—slammed on his brakes and began hurriedly backing up into the Trent driveway to turn around.

PRAYER IS LIKE OPENING A WINDOW IN A ROOM THAT IS UNBEARABLY HOT. PRAYER BRINGS IN THE FRESH AIR OF HOPE AND COMFORT.

As Aunt Sally bent over to pick up her Sunday paper, she was blissfully unaware that a double-wheeled wrecker was about to back over her.

I receive a panicked call that morning from Uncle Max, describing the accident and asking whether I could meet him at Baylor Hospital. I raced down the Dallas/Forth Worth Turnpike and arrived at the hospital, where a despondent Uncle Max fell into my arms and informed me that Aunt Sally—on top of her massive injuries—had just suffered a heart attack.

We were told her life was hanging by a thread. As for Uncle Max, his life was also crumbling all around him. There wasn't anything I could do but hug him and weep with him.

Up until now, Uncle Max had steadfastly refused to talk about religion. He loved having me over for dinner on Sunday nights, but he made it clear that he didn't want me talking about my faith or my work with Young Life, a Christian campus group. He wasn't interested in anything that smacked of faith. He was a Columbia graduate who held a Ph.D. in library science and had married another Columbia University Ph.D. in library science. He and Aunt Sally had their books and their knowledge, and that's all they needed.

Until that Sunday, when their secure world fell apart.

I asked Uncle Max whether he would mind if I prayed for Aunt Sally. "Please do," he replied. "Please pray for her...and for me."

We found a quiet corner of the waiting room just outside the critical care ward where we prayed for his wife. I prayed that she would make it through surgery. I prayed that her heart would mend and become strong. I prayed for the doctors and nurses practicing their skills. I prayed for courage, healing, and hope for Uncle Max.

We waited two long days and even longer nights for an answer to that prayer. With each update from a doctor or nurse, however, we were given more to pray about in our little corner, not less. And then in Baylor Hospital there came a resurrection day of sorts on the third day of waiting. Aunt Sally's primary physician unexpectedly came into the waiting room and asked for Uncle Max.

The news was nothing short of miraculous.

The doctor said that Aunt Sally was now responding in a way that shocked him. He felt he could confidently say she would not only pull through the heart surgery, but that she would be home within a month. (Turns out, she would beat that prognostication by a full week.)

When Uncle Max and I received that wonderful news, we hugged and cried, and then I prayed one more time with him. I thanked the Lord for what we both felt He had done through the surgeon's hands. And then Uncle Max asked me a question that would lead to a changed life for him. He asked, "Would you tell me more about this God we've been praying to?"

Would I? Of course I would! Yet it wasn't my words, but Uncle Max's desire to go to God in his time of need that led to a personal faith in Christ.

Prayer isn't a talisman. It's not a lucky charm. Did you know there was a time when Jesus prayed and received a "no" for an answer? It happened on the night before He gave up His life, when Jesus looked up and said, "Father, if You are willing, remove this cup from Me." He asked in agony and sorrow as He waited in the Garden. Even though the answer was no, He said, "Yet not My will, but Yours be done" (Luke 22:42).

Even if the answer to our prayers is no, we still grow closer to God when we pray. And we also grow closer as a family when we make prayer a part of our days and a constant practice in our homes.

Bedtime Blessings

Ever since our children were born, Cindy and I have prayed with them and over them at night. When Kari was only five years old, we used to wake her up in the morning with a homemade "blessing prayer."

The little singing prayer started, "Good morning, good morning, how are you today? The Lord bless you and keep you, throughout the day." It may not read like much, but this children's song sounded great when Cindy sang it. Soon this became our daughter's most requested song in the morning.

While Kari was normally a great sleeper, one time we were having trouble getting her to stay in her bed and go to sleep. We'd done a story and a prayer, a prayer and a story, water, a bathroom visit, one more story, one more glass of water, and then a last, last prayer. Finally, she was lovingly but firmly told that was it. No more games. No more stories. Time for bed. As we walked down the hall, convinced we had made our point, Kari made one last parting shot: "Good night, Mom, good night, Dad, and don't forget to bless me in the morning!"

It's hard to be angry with a kid who is asking you not to forget to pray for her in the morning, even if it's just a little song that sounds good only when Mom sings it. When you build prayer into your child's life, at mealtimes or bedtime or anytime, it makes a positive, lasting impression on him or her.

Whether it's prayer in a time of need, or prayer built into the DNA of our own or our children's daily lives, it can and does light up homes and lives.

We are living in a time when our prayers need to convey our need for God. One of the best verses that accomplishes that is 2 Chronicles 7:14, which says, "And [if] My people who are called by My name humble themselves and pray and seek My face and turn from their wicked ways, then I will hear from heaven, will forgive their sin and will heal their land."

Our land needs healing from within and without, and that begins with a prayerful and repentant heart. The Scriptures declare that there is an appointed time for everything—a time for every event under heaven (Ecclesiastes 3:1). I can't help but think that we are living in times that call for prayer and lots of it.

Prayer pulls a family together, a community together, and a nation together.

For now, more than ever, we need to be a people of prayer.

Making Your Family Stronger

I love something President Teddy Roosevelt said about himself. Immediately after taking up residence at the White House, Roosevelt asked Booker T. Washington to dinner. Afterward he was slammed in the press by racial critics who thought he was wrong to have invited this noted black inventor to dinner. Roosevelt dismissed their charges with the words, "If I have erred, I err in company with Abraham Lincoln." And then he went on to say, "I am only an average man, but by George, I work harder at it than the average man!"

What does that story have to do with living out a life of prayer? Actually, I think a great deal. For prayer is where presidents and pastors and everyday people and couples and parents gain the strength to stand against the wrongs of critics and the prejudice of our times. We may be just an "average" person, but it is when we pray that we find God's heart and really begin to understand how much Jesus loves us. And while prayer sustains us, it's when "average" people work harder at being more than "average" people of prayer that great things can happen in our family, communities, and country.

What should you pray about? For one thing, how about a family reunion? In a recent special on television, an investigative reporter looked into the burgeoning reunion industry. It seems that all across the country, family reunions are more popular than ever—so much so that hotels and airlines and other venders are cashing in on this growing craze to connect people with extended family.

Family reunions connect us with our past and with those we share much (even DNA) in common with. But I'm actually suggesting you pray about a different kind of "family reunion." It's pictured in these words,

I saw a new heaven and a new earth; for the first heaven and the first earth passed away...And I heard a loud voice from the throne, saying, "Behold, the tabernacle of God is among men, and He will dwell among them, and they shall be His people, and God Himself will be among them, and He will wipe away every tear from their eyes; and there will no longer be any death; there will no longer be any mourning, or crying or pain" (Revelation 21:1,3-4).

That's a picture of what those who love the Lord will one day see when "heaven comes down" and God's glory fills the earth. That will be a day of rejoicing with no pain, no death, no last goodbyes to beloved family members. That's something that's worth praying about each day.

And as we wait for the Lord's return, and the lion to indeed lay down with the lamb, my prayer for each of you is that you would take some of the thoughts and insights you've learned in these pages and prayerfully go out and find that "one family" we talked about at the beginning of this book. For to be a "Home of Light," it's time now to pray about which family you could come alongside. Not to lecture or scold, but to encourage and help them become a strong family themselves.

Can you imagine the power in a family, coming alongside just one other home that needs help? It's my prayer that in the days to come, one million families will read this book, perhaps take online courses at our

StrongFamily University site at www.strongfamilies.com, and most of all reach out with God's love to one other home in need.

May the Lord bless you and turn your home into a "Home of Light."

Closing Thoughts:
LIVING THE LIGHT OF HOME

*J*hope you've enjoyed and been challenged by the ten "word pictures" of a strong family in this book. As I close, I'd like to draw your thoughts to an outstanding painter, Claude Monet.

Many people have heard of Monet, perhaps the most famous impressionist painter of his day. Not a "starving artist," Monet lived with his wife and children in a palatial estate in the French countryside. Even today, Monet's gardens are considered some of the most beautiful in all of Europe. It was inside those garden walls that Monet captured on canvas most of his beautiful, peaceful masterpieces. Yet many may be unaware that these tranquil, inspiring scenes were painted during 1913-1918 amid the pain and darkness of World War I. While Monet was in his garden painting, thousands of men were marching by his estate. And like distant thunder, nearby constant artillery and machine gun fire could be heard from where his easel would have stood. That's because his peaceful gardens were less than three miles from the terrible trenches where over one million men died in battle.

In these dark days we live in, full of terror and war and heroism and grief, it's still possible to paint pictures of love and caring and commitment and warmth. They can be painted in the kitchens, rooms, hallways, and backyards of our homes. Our own masterpieces are waiting to be painted in lives lived well, where marriage vows are cherished, friendships are secured, seniors are honored, and children are raised in safety, security, and love. In fact, it's not only possible, it's essential that we choose to paint these pictures. For the light of home—the light of a home full of love and hope and caring and especially faith—is indeed an unstoppable way to push back the darkness.

Dr. John Trent
President, StrongFamilies.com

Let's Talk About It

$\mathcal{T}$he following questions are merely a guide to a deeper discussion of the material presented in each "picture" in the book. Whether you answer them privately or in a group setting, it is our prayer that God will use these questions to bless and strengthen your life and family.

Opening Thoughts: The Choice We Must Make

1. In your workplace, what changes have you seen since 9/11? In your family, what changes have you made or seen in this age of terrorism?

2. Dr. Trent talks about the need to see "pictures" of a strong family. In your own home growing up, what kind of "pictures" did you see? Were they of a close-knit, loving home, or pictures of strife and distance?

3. Is there one family you've watched over the years that models what you would picture as a strong family? What is it you see in their home that makes you pick them?

4. Do you agree with President Bush's quote, "Strong families make a strong America"? Why or why not?

5. Throughout this book, you'll come across the term "Homes of Light." As part of Dr. Trent's ministry, he's encouraging families across the country to commit to becoming a "Home of Light." That begins with a simple commitment at www.strongfamilies.com. And while it doesn't mean people have a perfect family, it's a statement that they are committed to learning and growing in their love for each other and the Lord. But a "Home of Light" doesn't end there. Committing to be a "Home of Light" also means walking across the street and helping at least one other family in need of encouragement and hope. For more information, visit www.strongfamilies.com.

The First Picture—Untying the Knots

1. When you read the story of the pastor who was asked by his daughter if he'd "visit" his own family, did it bring back memories of your childhood? Were your parents "there" for you at key times, or did you long for a level of connection that wasn't there?

2. Dr. Trent talked about the need to "untie the knot" (which is the literal translation of the Greek word to "set free"). Can you think of a person you struggled to forgive? In what ways does *not* forgiving a person "tie us in knots"?

3. The words "I'm sorry" were discussed as being key words in a strong family. In your opinion, why is it so hard to admit it when we're wrong—especially to family members?

4. Is there someone in your family, right now, that you need to forgive and—at least in your heart—"untie the knot"?

The Second Picture—Carving Out Time for Closeness

1. Was this the first time you had read the story of Michelangelo's David having been carved in snow before it was cut out of marble? Why do you think such a story could have such a powerful effect on a struggling couple like the one Dr. Trent met with that day?

2. Do you feel as though you're carving in snow when it comes to your marriage or family? Are you worried that the next time things "heat up" all your hard work will melt away? Have you shared that with your spouse? A close friend or relative? Your pastor or a God-honoring counselor? (If you'd like our prayer team at StrongFamilies.com to pray that all

your efforts will turn into "marble," please contact us at www.strongfamilies.com.)

3. Dr. Trent links a strong relationship with God as a key to "carving out commitment." Why is our commitment to the Lord such a powerful force when it comes to helping couples stay together instead of walking away?

The Third Picture—A Marriage Marked by Serving and Sharing

1. Cindy Trent felt "put on the shelf." Have you ever felt that way? Did you share your concern with your spouse? How did they respond? How should you respond if your spouse came to you and said they felt "put on the shelf" by you?

2. Do you agree with Dr. Trent's assertion that society (and movies) teach about courtship, not commitment? From your perspective, how has that helped or hurt those entering marriage?

3. "Having a strong marriage is hard work. Once you accept that fact, it becomes easier." What do you think of that quote from the book? What happens internally, emotionally, or spiritually when someone accepts this fact?

4. Dr. Trent also challenges couples to look at their marriage as their second "full-time job." While raising the children or going to work may be their main "job," working at their marriage is imperative. If you are married, discuss this question with your spouse: Does looking at marriage as a job take away from romance and intimacy?

The Fourth Picture—"Being There" for Our Children

1. Do you agree with the University of Dartmouth Medical School researcher that parents "overrate the rebelliousness of teenagers" and are more influential than they think? Why or why not?

2. Dr. Trent then challenges us to take the risk to "be there" for our children. Putting our "name" on our child carries the idea of marking them as special, valuable, priceless. When you were a child, did you have a parent, grandparent, or other person who "put their name" on you? (Saw tremendous value in you?) Do you think the children in your life feel that way in the way you talk to and treat them?

3. Putting our "eyes" on a child means looking for the best in their life. How long has it been since you made up a list of things you appreciate about your child—and read it to them?

4. Having our heart go out to a child is a beautiful picture of the need to relate to them at a heart level.

Try to understand the "need" behind their "deed." The feelings they carry. The hopes or dreams they have. Is this something you are regularly doing or could make a special effort to work toward?

5. There is a tough side to loving a child that Dr. Trent touches on in the story of how his mother refused to let him lock the door to his room. Is it a natural strength of yours to inspect and keep your child lovingly accountable, or is that a struggle?

The Fifth Picture—Affirming Courage in Our Children

1. "It is important for our sons and daughters to learn how to show courage under fire, even in life's small battles." Can you think of a time when a parent, coach, teacher, or friend affirmed you for being courageous in some way?

2. Turn up the sensitivity meter in your home and look to see what acts of kindness, service, integrity, or honor your child does that you could praise. It's the old, "Catch them doing something right and praise them for it" truism that can help affirm your child's stand that took courage or sacrifice.

3. Rent and watch *To Kill a Mockingbird* in the old black-and-white version as a family. After the movie, talk about what courage is as depicted in that movie—and how it can affect an entire family.

The Sixth Picture—Reconciling Relationships

1. We're talking about the need for forgiveness again in order to have a strong family. Only this time, let's focus on "closing the loop" on a past hurt we experienced with someone else. Can you think of an "open loop" incident in your life that has been like wearing "ankle weights"?

2. "If we're serious about having strong families, we must be free to move forward in life." The apostle John tells us that if there is hate in our life, we will walk in darkness (see 1 John 2:9,11). Do you have hate toward anyone you need to let go of so that you can walk in the Light?

3. For Dr. Trent, letting go of his hate and choosing instead to forgive was the act that allowed him to "close the loop" in his relationship with his father. Is there a key relationship you have that could use some forgiveness?

The Seventh Picture—Valuing and Listening to Our Seniors

1. Can you think of a relationship where you just knew you should talk to a loved one—and that window closed with their passing? In your opinion, why is it such a challenge to carve out time to talk to our seniors?

2. Proverbs 20:5 says, "The plan in the heart of a man is like deep water, but a man of understanding draws it out." Apply this verse to our seniors. What can you do to "draw out" the wisdom, life experience, and memories of a senior family member you love? Can you see how beneficial it would be—to you and them—if you did?

3. Dr. Trent shared how the loss of his grandfather, with so many unspoken words between them, motivated him to "draw deeply" from his grandmother, aunts, and mother. Is honoring and listening to the seniors in your life something you're teaching and modeling for your children?

The Eighth Picture—Remembering to Smile

1. In the touching story of a Marine, we can see the power of a smile and a simple act of kindness. While perhaps not as dramatic, can you think of a time when a small, unexpected act of kindness lifted your heart and spirits?

2. Being able to smile is a great American characteristic, even in the face of trials. What's the difference between "blind optimism" and a positive choice to "smile at the future"?

3. Dr. Trent also points out that laughter is a by-product of a close relationship with God. "You will make known to me the path of life; in Your presence is fullness of joy" (Psalm 16:11). Why is there

such a correlation between being close to the Lord and experiencing a joyful life? (Think about things like forgiveness, eternal life, unconditional acceptance, guidelines for successful living, and so on.)

The Ninth Picture—Opening Our Eyes to a Strong Faith

1. In an actual "thriller" that occurred in biblical times, Elisha prays for his fearful servant and asks Almighty God to open his eyes that he may see. "And the Lord opened the servant's eyes and he saw..." (2 Kings 6:17). Can you think of an Elisha-type friend who was instrumental in praying that your eyes would be opened to Christ and spiritual things? Have you thanked them lately?

2. Faith in the Bible is defined as the "conviction of things not seen" (Hebrews 11:1). There's that idea of seeing God's presence and reality beyond what we can see with the naked eye. Is there something you're struggling with trusting God for right now because you can't "see" a positive end or outcome?

3. Dr. Trent urges readers to find someone whose life is an example of faith and love for God and their family and follow them to their church. Do you have an outstanding church home? If you don't, is it time you asked a friend if you can follow them to church this coming Sunday?

The Tenth Picture—Becoming People of Prayer

1. Do you agree with the scientific conclusion that people are "hardwired" to believe in God? Why or why not?

2. In the story of Dr. Trent's Uncle Max, he and his wife built their life solely around each other. (They didn't believe in God, nor did they have children or anyone other than themselves.) From this story, or your own story or observations, why is it so important to have a strong faith before and especially when trials come?

3. Specifically talking about prayer, Dr. Trent shares a "no" answer to Jesus' prayer in the Garden of Gethsemane. Instead of shattering His faith, Jesus said, "Not what I will, but what You will" (Mark 14:32) and headed to the cross. Are you struggling with a "no" answer to one of your prayers? Is there an example and lesson here that can strengthen your faith?

4. Now, more than ever, we need to be a people of prayer. If you're a novice when it comes to prayer, spend some time reading the Lord's Prayer (Luke 11:2-4) and Psalm 23. Both of these wonderful sections of Scripture can be templates for interaction with Almighty God.

5. Dr. Trent mentioned how he and his wife prayed with and for their daughters every night. Is that a small, specific thing you can start to do to make prayer more a part of your strong family?

A Special Invitation from Dr. Trent to Our Readers

This book launches a national campaign to strengthen home and families across our country. Our goal is to see one million families sign up as "Homes of Light" and become lighthouses for their neighborhoods, churches, communities, and country. We invite you to visit www.strongfamilies.com, where you can sign up as a "Home of Light"; receive a free weekly E-zine filled with practical help and hope; find out about Strong Families seminars; take online premarital, marriage, and parenting courses; and take the "Leading from Your Strengths" online strength assessment.

NOTES

1. Gustave le Bon, *The Crowd: A Study of the Popular Mind,* quoted in Roy H. Williams, "When We All Think As One" in the online *Monday Morning Memo,* September 24, 2001. Italics are added for emphasis by Dr. Trent.

2. From "Ministry Essentials," by Charles Swindoll, Ministry Essentials conference 1994, Dallas Theological Seminary.

3. Adam Schefter, "Plummer Getting Set for Scrutiny," *Denver Post* (August 8, 2003). Italics added for emphasis by Dr. Trent.

4. Associated Press article in *The Arizona Republic,* December 3, 2001, "Study Says Parents Can Dissuade Kids from Smoking," quoting from *Pediatrics,* December 2001.

5. If you are interested in this assessment, please go to www.strongfamilies.com and click on "Discover Your Unique God-given Strengths" next to the four boxes of animals. Please follow the prompts from there. To cover the costs of providing the report, there is a charge for the assessment.

6. Michael Schol and Tom Spain, eds., "Miracle on a Train," in *I'll Be Home for Christmas: The Library of Congress Revisits the Spirit of Christmas During World War II* (New York: Delacorte Press, 1999), pages 127-31. "Miracle on a Train" was originally published as: Edward Andrusko, "Welcome Home and Merry Christmas," in *Navy Times,* December 19, 1997. Used by permission.

7. Ibid., p. 127.

8. Ibid., p. 130.

9. Ibid., p. 131.

10. If you need some help with this exercise, I have written a book called *Life Mapping* (Colorado Springs: Waterbrook Press, 2000). You can find a copy at your local Christian bookstore or at www.strongfamilies.com.

Other Harvest House Reading

The Power of a Praying® Parent
by *Stormie Omartian*

Popular author and singer Stormie Omartian offers 30 easy–to–read chapters that focus on specific areas of prayers for parents. This personal, practical guide leads the way to enriched, strong prayer lives for parents.

A Woman After God's Own Heart®
by *Elizabeth George*

Scripture–based principles for every reader who wants to become God's woman of excellence. For any woman who wants to achieve a growing relationship with God, develop an active partnership with her husband, and make her home into a spiritual oasis. Study guide included.

A Man After God's Own Heart®
by *Jim George*

Many Christian men want to be a man after God's own heart…but how do they become one? Author Jim George shows that a heartfelt desire to grow spiritually is all that's needed. God's grace does the rest—bringing lasting change to a man's heart.

365 Things Every New Mom Should Know
by *Linda Danis*

This daily guide to the first year of motherhood combines prayerful, playful, and practical information to energize new moms. Features weekly devotionals and daily activities that foster a baby's physical, emotional, social, and spiritual growth.

Survival Guide for New Dads
by *Nick Harrison* and *Steve Miller*

First-time fathers are often intimidated by their new role, but they need not fear! This helpful guide provides 90 inspirational devotions, each based on Scripture and rich with practical advice.